EARTHEN
LONG BARROWS

THE EARLIEST MONUMENTS IN THE BRITISH ISLES

EARTHEN LONG BARROWS

THE EARLIEST MONUMENTS IN THE BRITISH ISLES

DAVID FIELD

The
History
Press

First published by Tempus Publishing in 2006

Reprinted in 2016 by
The History Press
The Mill, Brimscombe Port,
Stroud, Gloucestershire, GL5 2QG

British Library Cataloguing in Publication Data.
A catalogue record for this book is available from the British Library.

ISBN 978 0 7524 4013 2

Typesetting and origination by Tempus Publishing Limited
Printed in Great Britain

CONTENTS

ILLUSTRATIONS

MONOCHROME FIGURES

COLOUR PLATES

PREFACE

White Barrow, situated at the heart of Salisbury Plain, is a trapezoidal mound of enormous bulk. It has certainly attracted its share of early investigation, but the Bronze Age linear ditches that surround it on three sides are now supplemented by fences in order to protect it from marauding tanks. Cared for by the National Trust on an island surrounded by military land, the major concern of recent years has been to convince the badgers that they would prefer a custom made set a little distance away. Having seen off antiquarians and soldiers, the mound now nestles peacefully among the trees that mark the site. Recent geophysical work by English Heritage produced useful details of construction, highlighting the presence of a trapezoidal mortuary enclosure with an arc of pits or postholes at the eastern end (Payne 2000). That is only appropriate, for White Barrow was one of the first long barrows to be recognised and recorded. John Aubrey, presumably *en route* from his home at Easton Piercy to farm at Broad Chalke, perceptively observed that the massive mound was associated with a series of linear ditches (Fowles (ed.) 1980, 712) and indeed added the site to his inventory.

Aubrey's childhood home at Easton Piercy, now a small hamlet near Chippenham in north Wiltshire, thus features prominently in the search for origins, for here during the earlier part of the seventeenth century, 'before the civill warres', he soaked up influences from land and people and attained a deep-rooted affinity with the past. Perhaps better known for his descriptions of the lives of his famous contemporaries and for introducing King Charles II to the monuments at Avebury, it was in fact Aubury who was the first to closely observe and record the presence of long barrows. Almost certainly the local environment influenced his views. Born here in 1626, the medieval village may have already been deserted, leaving the earthworks and old house stances as a playground, for Aubrey described his isolation from other children, being brought up in a 'kind of Parke' (the outline of which can still be traced on the modern map). Beyond it were the earthworks and remains of St Mary's Priory, which seems to have influenced his admiration for these monastic institutions that had been broken up almost within local memory. He was aware that those in the neighbourhood: Stanley Abbey, Farleigh Abbey, Malmesbury Abbey, all abounded with monuments, relics and manuscripts and offered a tangible link with the past (Jackson (ed.) 1862, 4). Deprived of education at the Priory by events in a previous century, he went to school at the local church in Leigh Delamare, a place now well-known as a service station on the M4 motorway and which unfortunately bisects the church from its catchment. His journeys around the local countryside not only ensured familiarity with the ruins of the recent past, but earlier remains as well. Within a short compass were long mounds at Lugbury, Nettleton and Lanhill, near Chippenham, and the Giant's Cave near Malmesbury, all of which he recorded and made drawings of. He studied the principles of geometry and 'having a quick draught, have drawn landskips on horseback symbolically' (Dick 1949, 101). A family property at Broad Chalke in south Wiltshire ensured journeys across Salisbury Plain and as a result he became familiar with the area around Stonehenge from an early age, subsequently noting the presence of between 43 and 45 barrows in the vicinity (there are in fact many more).

While visiting Silbury Hill in 1658, King Charles II asked him to prepare a description of Avebury and, in addition, the Duke of York required 'an account of the Old Camps and Barrows on the Plaines' (Dick 1949, 69). Having observed the deficiencies in Inigo Jones study of Stonehenge he resolved to present plans of both it and Avebury and, probably using a plane table, in September 1663 prepared and presented the first measured survey of those monuments. In doing so he highlighted the circle of pits – later called the Aubrey holes – at Stonehenge and the angular nature of the earthworks at Avebury (Welfare 1989) subsequently ignored by Stukeley and other cartographers. This acute observation of the subtleties of earthworks, presumably stimulated by those undulations around his childhood home, served him well and it was this that allowed him to appreciably comment on the earthworks around White Barrow. He was aware of the effect and importance that local construction materials would have and suggested that Boles Barrow might be made of local flint nodules (Fowles (ed.) 1980, 712).

Aubrey's journeys on the downs between 1665 and 1693 allowed him to record the presence of long mounds at Winterbourne Monkton (Millbarrow), West Kennet and an unknown mound on an unnamed down 'about a mile westward from Marlborough', but which would place it at Manton. All of these were depicted with standing stones placed around their perimeter, 20 at the latter site, 29 at Millbarrow, while West Kennet was depicted with chambers, or at least a tumble of sarsens close to or at the wider end (Fowles (ed.) 1980, 802-812).

In the centuries to follow, William Stukeley and particularly William Cunnington, both investigated the interior of the mounds and established a line of archaeological enquiry that has still not run its course. While they may represent the grandfather and father respectively of long barrow studies, Aubrey was the instigator who outlined the potential.

Long barrows, single mounds of earth flanked by ditches, are our earliest of monuments, with dates frequently in the first quarter of the fourth millennium BC and, as such, are an obvious source of enquiry for the origins of our farming lifestyle. Long considered to be burial monuments, sometimes of chieftains or of those killed during warfare, and more recently as markers of good pasture or agricultural land (Renfrew 1973: Chapman 1981), their true purpose still eludes us and the detail of modern excavation has only provided greater fascination. Some contain no burials at all, others the remains of up to about 50 people. Some mounds are massive and monumental, others more subtle and easily overlooked. Some are divided into cells or stalls, yet others are built almost entirely of turf. This book will investigate this variety and complexity and will address problems of function and how perceptions may have changed over time. As will become apparent, it is very much written from the field archaeology perspective and the emphasis falls heavily on Wessex examples with which the writer is most familiar. It differs markedly from both Paul Ashbee's invaluable *The Earthen Long Barrow in Britain*, which ran to two editions, and has been out of print for some time now, and Ian Kinnes' important and comprehensive treatment which is aimed mainly at academics. More recently, Tim Darvill's excellent reworking of O.G.S. Crawford's *The Long Barrows of the Cotswolds* published by Tempus has provided a modern perspective of that group of monuments and consequently discussion of the Severn/Cotswold group is avoided here. In any event, many of those barrows contain stone chambers or have mounds constructed of stones (cairns) and, although related, fall into a slightly different category. Since first publication of this book important and comprehensive reports have appeared on the Ascott-under-Wychwood long cairn in Oxfordshire by Don Benson and Alasdair Whittle and others (2006), the Haddenam long barrow, Cambridgeshire, by Christopher Evans and Ian Hodder (2006), Whiteleaf, Buckinghamshire by Gill Hey and colleagues (2007) and, critically, an important report on the dating and chronology of long barrows by Alex Bayliss and Alasdair Whittle (2007). In addition work on the dating of causewayed enclosures by Alasdair Whittle, Alex Bayliss and Frances Healy (2011) has had significant impact on the subject. Without doubt, these articles and volumes, in particular those on dating, have been among the most important developments in long barrow studies. Use of Bayesian statistics applied to radiocarbon 14 determinations in archeology has now become quite standard practise and is routinely applied to sites of all periods.

Programmes of analysis on human bone have also taken place and assesments made of the amount of disease, the extent of violent activities and other skeletal conditions (Smith and Brickley 2009). This volume avoids that ground. Instead, it aims to provide new perspectives for the general reader; a perspective grounded in the importance of the land.

No fresh excavations have been conducted at earthen long barrows during the last decade, but the result of investigations by Oxford Archeology at the kidney shaped mound at Whiteleaf originally excavated by Lindsay Scott in the 1930s have indicated that it has a U-shaped ditch and was originally of Cranborne Chase type, the once oval mound probably being deformed by Bronze Age or Roman-British diggers. The single burial found by Scott was assessed to have been placed between two posts and dated to 2760-3640 BC and the mound constructed intermittently with episodes dated to 3660-3520 and 3370-3100 (Hey *et al* 2007).

Some illustrations, particularly of excavation plans, have been redrawn and sometimes simplified in order to provide consistency of style, metric scales, and highlight points of comparison, but those readers interested in further research are always encouraged to return to the originals just in case minor detail has been omitted. Dates are expressed as calibrated date ranges in calendar years at 95per cent probability using the OxCal 3.9 programme. Plans and illustrations depict mounds oriented with north at the top of the page except where indicated by a north arrow.

Often obscured by hedgerows or old coppices out in the countryside and invariably at a distance from habitation, long barrows still retain the air of mystery and sense of the past that intrigued John Aubrey. Some are absolutely enormous, yet constructed without the aid of metal tools. Others so subtle that they appear as sculpture-like art forms that blends perfectly with the landscape. They beckon enquiry and demand investigation. What follows is an attempt at doing that.

ACKNOWLEDGEMENTS

I would like to thank my colleagues in the former RCHME and in English Heritage with whom I have spent much pleasant time visiting, surveying and analysing barrows, struggling with the intricacies of the earthworks and becoming fully engaged with each monument. Every few years one of those 'eureka' moments occurs, when several things fall into place at once. Graham Brown, Dave McOmish, Deborah Cunliffe, Pete Topping, have all shared in this. Other colleagues, Nicky Smith, Mark Bowden, Dilwyn Jones, Peter Horne and David MacLeod have all provided influence as has Damian Grady and Martyn Barber. Encouraged to publish our work, Pete Topping, Head of Archeological Survey and now at the University of Newcastle, kindly read through an earlier draft of the text at a time when it was in an appalling condition and sanctioned use of images, while Graham Brown scanned the pages for things out of place. Ros Cleal at the Alexander Keiller Museum, Janet Bell at the Salisbury and South Wiltshire Museum, David Allen at the Hampshire Museums and Archive Service and Paul Robinson at Wiltshire Heritage Museum, Devizes, were extremely helpful in providing some of the illustrations or access to the material, while Ian Leonard assisted with finds from South Street. The cover illustration, a reconstruction of the Nutbane long barrow by Mike Codd is provided courtesy of Hampshire County Council Museums and Archive Service. Unacknowledged illustrations are the work of the author. Paul Ashbee very kindly allowed his illustrative material to be used and provided welcome encouragement. I would also like to thank Ian Kinnes for past discussions about long barrows and Richard Bradley for more recent ones and last but by no means least, Christine and Catherine for being patient during days spent at the computer, or visiting 'yet another long barrow'.

1

THE FIRST MONUMENTS

NEOLITHIC BACKGROUND

Among the earliest Neolithic artefacts to be found in Britain are a series of cut, ground and polished axes made of jadeitite, at least some of which are thought to have originated from sources in the Italian Alps. They are found across the UK, from Scotland to the south coast of England, but often adjacent to the communication corridors, the rivers and streams that provided focus for well-established communities exploiting the drainage basins. The superb axe from Breamore in Hampshire (*1*) is typical, the template, long and thin with a pointed butt, similar to those found on the mainland of Europe in the Paris Basin or around Carnac. A similar axe was found associated with the Sweet Track, a well-constructed wooden trackway built through marshland in Somerset, which was dated by dendrochronology to 3806 BC and which carries with it implications that monitoring of the local woodland and countryside was taking place by that time. The Sweet Track axe may well be older than that, for it is the type of artefact that might be curated and passed down through generations. This simply broadens the interpretation, either of an earlier dispersion to the British Isles, or of importation after having been curated for generations elsewhere. However, the common origin of this and similar axes found across Europe, helps demonstrate the enormous extent of a sphere of contact and influence where ideas and innovation might mature and evolve. Within such an area local customs and behaviour, in turn influenced by geographies, climate and indigenous tradition will have prospered and led to a shared repertoire of cultural themes reflected in architecture and material possessions.

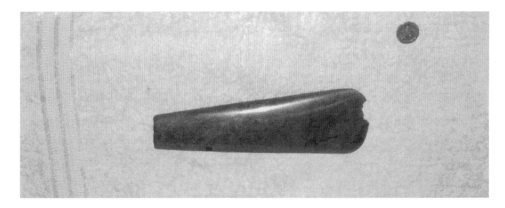

1 Jadeitite axe found at Breamore, in the Avon valley, Hampshire, made of material probably originating in the Italian Alps. *Courtesy of the Wiltshire Heritage Museum, Devizes*

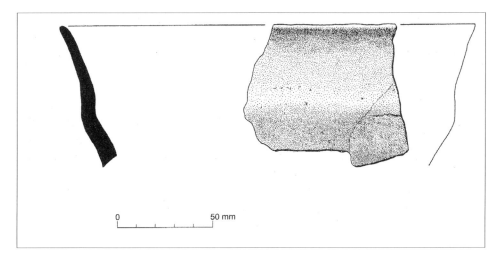

2 Fragment of early Neolithic 'Grimston Ware' bowl from a flint mine shaft at Cissbury, Sussex, recovered during Lane Fox's excavations in 1867. *Pitt Rivers Museum, Oxford: drawing Field and Pearson*

CHRONOLOGY

Pointed-butt ground axes were certainly present in Britain from around, if not before, the turn of the fourth millennium BC. An example made of flint and dated to 4250–3980 cal. BC was recovered from deposits in a massive natural shaft at Down Farm, Sixpenny Handley, Dorset (Green and Allen: French *et al* 2007, fig A4.2); while a further ground-flint axe now dated to the 38th century BC (Richards 1990, 259: Barclay 2014), was recovered from a pit named the Coneybury Anomaly, near Stonehenge in Wiltshire. In contrast to the other flint tools from the same context, the latter was of a grey flint very characteristic of mined material. It would hardly be surprising if it turned out to be so, as the few available radiocarbon estimates for the well-known Neolithic flint mines in Sussex and Hampshire also indicate an origin around the turn of the millennium. These are often single dates on bone or antler from old excavations and should be treated with due caution, but there is a degree of consistency about them and incidental supporting evidence of, for example, a carinated bowl considered to be an early form which was found in one of the flint-mine shafts at Cissbury (2). There are also signs of early extraction at some rock extraction sites; for example, a single date of 4350-3990 cal. BC at Graiglwyd in north Wales (Williams *et al.* 1998) indicates that the rock may have been exploited for ground axes around the same time.

Deposits at the Down Farm shaft, as well as the Coneybury Anomaly, contained carinated western-style potsherds, while the latter site also produced a leaf-shaped flint arrowhead and cereal grains. Along with the presence of roe deer, cattle and a sheep-sized animal, this not only provides (cautiously slender) evidence for a mixed economy but, by implication, of an organised use of the land. It also indicates that those features generally considered representative of a Neolithic lifestyle were in use soon after the turn of the millennium if not considerably before. The nature of the cultivation may have been small scale, perhaps in gardens, but there is increasing evidence for it elsewhere in Britain. The large Neolithic building at Balbridie, Kincardineshire, has been – albeit controversially – interpreted as a grain store (Rowley-Conwy 2002), while grain has also been recovered from the Knap of Howar, in Orkney, from a riverside house at Lismore Fields, Derbyshire and what appeared to be a lump of bread recovered from a large house-like structure at Yarnton, Oxfordshire was dated to 3620-3350 cal. BC, rather later in the millennium (Anon 2001). The earliest recorded large cereal grain now dates to *c.* 3800 cal BC (Brown 2007).

Exactly when the 'Neolithic' lifestyle began is unclear. There is a sharp division between, on the one hand, recognisably Neolithic features, monuments and artefacts, which consistently date to the period after about 4000 BC, and flaked-flint tool assemblages which include microliths, but which date from an earlier time. The weathering cone of the Down Farm shaft trapped a succession of deposits that have been dated by radiocarbon assay. A series of microliths of which five were of a diagnostic 'rod' type, were dated by C14 taken from a *bos primigenus* bone to 4340-4040 cal. BC. While sites such as this dating to the fifth millennium are rare, wherever they are encountered the typical Neolithic tools are absent. However, mundane types of flint tool: fabricators, denticulated pieces, scrapers, saws and pieces struck by using tranchet techniques, continue the trend established in the earlier period. Blades decline in length over time, but it is only the special types, arrowheads and ground axes that provide novelty; the new forms seemingly introduced over a short time span.

A recent dating programme using Bayesian analysis of radiocarbon dated events refined the dates of several long barrows (Bayliss & Whittle 2007). The complex method provides several modes for a sequence of events based on the nature of archaeology. The interpretation preferred by analysts indicate that burials were placed in a wooden mortuary structure at Fussell's Lodge around 3700, the structure extended around 3675-3640 cal BC, which corresponds with the construction of inner and outer ditches at the nearby causewayed structure at Wayland's Smithy around 3610-3550, the structure remaining accessible for about a generation before being mounded over around 3530-3435 cal BC. An episode of burning cleared the site around 3490-3390 cal BC following which the trapezoidal stone chambered mound visible today was constructed and use of the site finished by 3430-3265 cal BC. Other C14 determinations indicate that the first long barrows are present at around 3800-3700 cal. BC, but most dates place appearance a little before the middle of the millennium. This is 200-300 years after the introduction of new flint tools and pottery making, and before widespread introduction of causewayed enclosures. Whether this represents new beliefs in funerary matters or a concern with land possession will be explored below.

Taking the material from the Down Farm shaft into account, the evidence can be interpreted to support the idea of a period of technological change beginning about 4300 BC involving the introduction of new types of artefact, leaf-shaped arrowheads, ground axes and pottery, and the first arable cultivation, introduced over a period of perhaps 500 years. Alternatively, it can account for a rapid introduction of monuments, new artefact types and domestic animals around the turn of the fifth to fourth millennium as Rick Schulting (2000) has suggested. Both Terry Manby (1988) in his analysis of the material from Yorkshire and Alasdair Whittle (1993) who analysed the material from around Avebury, concluded that a period of lifestyle change occurred between about 4300 and 3900 BC. Manby suggested that this represented a pioneering phase, while Whittle envisaged that the first clearances were made at this time. It may have simply been new ideas as much as an influx of new people that were responsible, as rising sea-levels forced population movement and the crystallisation of new methods of subsistence. The sea-level rose by some 5m between about 5300 and 3000 cal. BC (data in Long & Roberts 1997, figs 12c & 13) inundating much of the low-lying landscape of the eastern and southern coasts, while today's narrow tidal range was established by about 4920-4780 cal. BC making former occupation and exploitation of a wide inter-tidal zone no longer possible. Any former reliance on marine resources had to be flexible as a population repeatedly found itself under pressure from changing coastal configuration.

The main causewayed enclosure at Hambledon Hill, a circuit of discontinuous banks and ditches, was constructed around 3650-3520 cal. BC; that at Whitesheet Hill around

3780-3380 and Windmill Hill 3650-3370 cal. BC (for more precision now see Whittle *et al* 2011). New pottery, both plain and decorated bowls, representing a mature or developed phase of the Neolithic was also introduced at this time. The intensity of this activity is marked and Ros Cleal (2004) has suggested that a 'horizon' of rapid change may signal the years 3600-3700 cal. BC. The mature Neolithic period then appears to last for *c.*500 years until around 3000 BC, when the circular earthworks at Stonehenge and Flagstones and, perhaps the first enclosure at Avebury were constructed. By this time many long barrows appear to have gone out of use, at least, the ditches had silted up and Mortlake Ware, with a date range of 3400 BC through to 2500 BC (Gibson and Kinnes 1997) appeared in secondary positions in the silted ditches. Alongside these events the construction of massive round barrows took place while new artefact types such as 'Seamer' series ground-flint axes and jet sliders, when found as burial associations appear to mark a change in the importance of the individual.

THE FIRST MONUMENTS

Long barrows, visible in the countryside as enormous mounds of earth anything up to about 100m in length, 35m wide and 4m high, are among the best known and easily recognised archaeological monuments in the landscape. Attempts to classify them based on certain attributes such as ditch plan have met with varied degrees of success though often the resultant typology has served to mask the range of different barrow types. Earthen long barrows, a term originally used by Stuart Piggott in preference to John Thurnam's 'unchambered', was used to distinguish from those that had a megalithic burial structure and was adopted at a time when he could point to a mere handful of excavated examples. The classification presents problems in that not all elements of barrows without stone chambers need be 'earthen'. Standing stones, a peristalith, or internal features such as earlier cairns or platforms of stone or flint, can and do often feature. In addition to 'earth' (usually combinations of soil, turf and soft rock such as chalk and sand), the mound itself might be made of various amounts of collected stones, making the distinction with cairns difficult.

When stone burial chambers stand proud of an eroded barrow as, for example, at Kits Coty House in Kent, the megalithic structure is clear, but it is less so where the mound survives intact: places such as Lanhill, Chippenham, Wiltshire (*3*), or Lodge Park, Gloucestershire (*4*), where two stones just breaking the surface provide the only clue to potential megalithic build.

Equally, typological separation according to the nature of the mound material may be illusory and mask important similarities, particularly in those located close to what might be considered a stone using area. This is particularly noticeable at Avebury, where the local sarsen boulders could be utilised and where limestone is available 10km away. It seems inevitable

3 Lanhill long barrow, near Chippenham, Wiltshire. John Thurnam discovered two stone chambers when he excavated here in 1855. A further chamber containing the remains of eleven individuals and consisting of six large stone slabs was subsequently found while men were digging out stone in 1909

that many of the construction materials simply reflect what was available in the immediate area: that, for example, many earthen mounds on the chalk utilised flint for building and that there will be uncertainty and overlap. In his comprehensive work on the subject, Ian Kinnes used the term non-megalithic barrows, as distinct from unchambered, thus excluding those with peristalith as well as stone chamber.

The National Monuments Record, perhaps wisely, does not distinguish between types or materials, and simply lists the presence of 538 definite and probable long barrows in England. In addition 102 mortuary enclosures and 14 bank barrows are listed. In Scotland at least 42 long mounds are known although a considerable number of these may be cairns.

More recently aerial photography has not only extended the known distribution, but also emphasised the potentially greater variety of related types of monuments. Increasingly, long enclosures are being recognised from the air. Dilwyn Jones (1998) has identified and analysed a series of long barrow related cropmarks in Lincolnshire, while Cathy Stoertz (RCHME 1997) has completed a similar study for the Yorkshire Wolds. Long mortuary enclosures, with or without covering mounds, are now generally recognised as an important and integral component of the architectural repertoire, while the uncertainty over whether bank barrows are more allied to long barrows or cursus monuments has not been resolved.

The long barrows are part of a wider range of monuments that can be found across Britain and Ireland and indeed much of Europe, many featuring common architectural components used in different combinations. In the west and north this includes various types of stone burial chambers covered with long mounds of stone usually referred to as cairns. In the south and east they are predominantly 'earthen'.

RECOGNITION

Long Barrows are relatively simple earthworks and there is much scope for misidentification, especially when any subtle ledges and breaks of slope, or

4 A long barrow in Lodge Park, Gloucestershire with parkland trees in the background. At the higher end of the mound, limestone boulders to one side may have been reconstructed as part of a landscaping exercise. *Photograph: N. Smith*

the ditches that might assist identification, have been obscured by episodes of cultivation. The major confusion is with coniger mounds or rabbit warrens, commonly referred to as 'pillow mounds', which are often similar in size and shape. The cluster of long pillow mounds inside Dolebury Warren hillfort in the Mendips are unmistakable as the remains of a Warrener's Lodge lies in attendance and in any case the place name urges caution. However, the example set on Hollybush spur within the Midsummer Hill hillfort in the Malvern Hills (5) has been mistaken for a long barrow. Close inspection reveals linear depressions along and across its summit resulting from collapsed rabbit tunnels and its real nature is not in doubt. Another long mound surrounded by a ditch at West Putford, Devon, identified from aerial photographs suspiciously contains an internal trench and is also likely to be a pillow mound.

Landscaping can also result in misidentification. Two mounds in Stoke Park, Bristol, were originally interpreted as long barrows, but when one was excavated by the Folk House Archaeological Club in 1954/5 and medieval pottery recovered from close to the old ground surface, it became clear that they were associated with the designed landscape of the park.

A further earthwork that can be confused is the rifle butt, usually sculpted into a hillslope, although when on level ground they can easily be misinterpreted as long barrows. The Queens Butt on Wimbledon Common, London (Johnson and Wright 1903, 68: MacDonald 1976, 19) may be an example and one such mound lies adjacent to a genuine long barrow at Tilshead, in Wiltshire.

Cultivation can very easily disfigure and disguise mounds, especially shallow ones. Partly levelled long mounds can be mistaken for oval or round mounds. The process of denudation might even have been an ancient one. At Middleton Down, in Wiltshire, for example, the presence of 'Celtic' fields indicates that damage might have taken place during prehistory or the Roman period (6).

The large mound on Windover Hill in Sussex reaches 68m in length with a level summit at a height of 2m and was identified and surveyed as a possible long barrow by Herbert S. Toms (1922) who had formerly been surveyor to Lt General Pitt Rivers on Cranborne Chase. It is surrounded by an area of chalk quarries and a cambered feature once thought to be a Roman Road leads upslope directly towards it. Inspected in greater detail by the Royal Commission of the Historical Monuments of England (RCHME) in recent years, the road is undoubtedly a tramway associated with the quarry and the long barrow a terminal associated with it (*colour plate 1*). It remains possible that the quarry workers modified and utilised an existing mound, but they could equally have constructed a brand new one. Unfortunately there is little direct

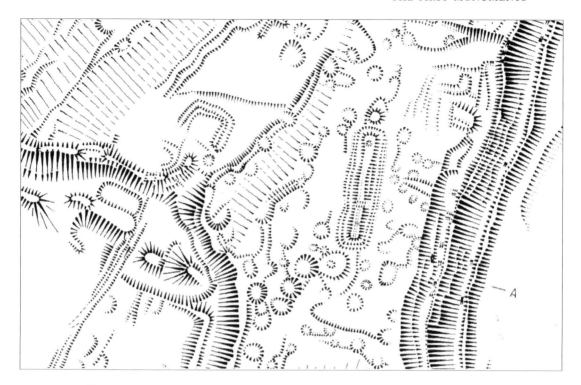

5 A pillow mound set amongst the earthworks of Midsummer Hill Iron Age hillfort on the summit of the Malvern Hills in Herefordshire. The mound is markedly rectangular with a sharp-profiled ditch surrounding it. Shallow depressions on the summit of the mound betray where tunnels created to encourage rabbits have collapsed and sunk. © *Crown copyright NMR*

evidence that this should be so and extreme caution is now required regarding its true classification. Only excavation to test the nature of the mound will confirm the point.

In parts of the country formerly affected by glaciation, moraine deposits left on valley floors can easily be misinterpreted as long barrows. With one end higher and wider than the other and sometimes the odd boulder lying around as though it once formed a peristalith or chamber, only their large size can rule them out. One example, the 82m-long mound at Dunham New Park in Cheshire, formerly thought to be a long barrow and plotted on the Ordnance Survey map as such, is now thought to be a natural mound of glacial sand (Anon 1961). Similarly, excavation of a trapezoidal 50m long and 2.5m high mound at Coffee Pot Plantation, Hamsterley, Co. Durham in 1980 demonstrated that it was in fact a natural knoll (Young 1980). Conversely, it has been argued that a mound on Herald Hill, Aberdeenshire, formerly thought to be natural may be a genuine long barrow (Barclay and Maxwell 1998).

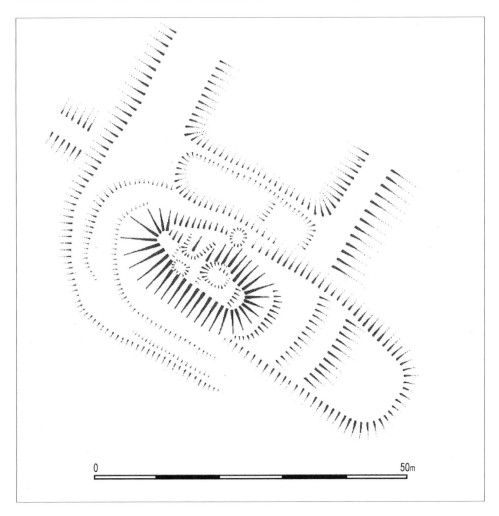

6 Plan of long barrow on Middleton Down, near Warminster in Wiltshire. 'Celtic' fields, probably dating from the Middle Bronze Age have encroached on and partially levelled the mound. © *Crown copyright NMR*

As if such difficulties of identification are not enough there is a problem with form as smaller long barrows have often been classified as round or oval barrows. In the mid-nineteenth century Thurnam excluded barrows from his study that were oval in plan as he considered them to be Bronze Age in date (Thurnam 1869: 1871), but excavation during the latter part of the twentieth century has demonstrated that they fall within the Neolithic period.

Frequently encountered are genuine Neolithic round barrows, both in stone and earthen materials and again widely distributed across northern Europe, some of which house stone burial chambers. In parts of the country they may masquerade as mounds of later date, especially where they have become part of a cemetery of mounds. Although some of these, the Boyne tombs in Ireland, or Maes Howe for example, or earthen mounds in Yorkshire such as Duggleby Howe, are quite massive constructions, others such as Handley 26 and 27 adjacent to Wor Barrow in Dorset are relatively small and easily overlooked. Ian Kinnes (1979) has highlighted the potential distribution of these mounds and demonstrated that some have a good early Neolithic pedigree. Some long mounds have tails attached, for example, that at Crickley Hill (Dixon 1988), or Longmanhill, Banffshire (Barclay and Maxwell 1998), but in other cases round barrows constructed over a long mound might give rise to spoon-shaped cropmarks, such as such as that at Ulceby, when levelled (Jones D. 1998).

One of the most intriguing and distinctive features of many long barrows is the trapezoidal plan. Even when only fragments, in particular the expanding ditches, are present on air photographs it is often enough to secure the identity of a site. The form is quite unusual and not easily explained, but is nevertheless widespread in England and elsewhere in Europe (7). It has been suggested that it derives from the form of Linearbandkeramik long houses of central Europe (Piggott 1966) or the ancestral memory of them (Bradley 2002).

In her analysis of Hampshire long barrows, Isobel Smith suggested that only mounds with side ditches should be considered as long barrows (RCHME 1979a), in so doing excluding what had become well-established sites such as West Rudham, Norfolk and Skendleby 1, Lincolnshire, although she made an exception to include the Thickthorn Down long barrow in Dorset. In his study, Ian Kinnes (1992) distinguished between trapezoidal, rectangular and ovoid mounds, with flanking side ditches, or U-form ditches that enclose one end, or that fully enclose the mound. These inclusive definitions broadened the category and is essentially the one used here (8).

Long barrows can certainly be distinguished as ditched mounds generally of 20–70m in length, but there are exceptional examples at both ends of the scale. Some reach beyond 100m, but to exclude such well-known monuments as West and East Kennet, Old Ditch and East Heslerton (*colour plate 2*) as long barrows and re-classify them as bank barrows may be inappropriate. At present the overlap with bank barrows, cursus monuments, long cairns and mortuary enclosures is considerable, suggesting that dimensions alone did not determine the nature of these monuments.

Long mortuary enclosures, long enclosed spaces defined by a ditch or palisade or some other construction, are known initially from the example on Normanton Down, where an extant enclosure was recognised as being similar to that excavated by Pitt Rivers beneath Wor Barrow in Dorset. Excavations at Dorchester by Richard Atkinson and at Fussell's Lodge by Paul Ashbee led

7 The trapezoidal long mound of Reisenburg, Isle of Rügen, Germany, revetted by a peristalith of glacially transported boulders

to the view that these enclosures were an integral part of the long barrow tradition (Piggott 1966). Aerial photographs have since demonstrated that with or without barrow coverings they are widespread and there are currently 102 listed in the National Monuments Record. Their size range lies between about 22m and 128m in length and 10m to 38m in width and it compares well with that of long barrows. Like long barrows they can be separated into ovoid (oval, curvilinear), trapezoidal (trapeziform) and rectangular (oblong) forms and it has been suggested that they form the lower end of a continuum of monuments incorporating cursuses, bank barrows and long barrows (Loveday and Petchey 1983). Uncertainty whether some fall into the bank barrow or short cursus category has led to the use of the term 'elongated enclosures' (Jones, D. 1998), the 'mortuary' element being dispensed with. I have retained it here for convenience as it is reasonably well ingrained in long barrow literature although that by no means should be understood to imply function.

Whereas long barrows rarely exceed about 70m in length, bank barrows are very much longer. The Maiden Castle example reaches 546m, but at the shorter end of the range Bradford Peverell is just 64m. Only 14 bank barrows are known in the record. Levelled examples recorded as cropmarks occur as parallel cursus-like ditches, but in all other respects they are indistinguishable from long barrows and it is only length that sets them apart. There must be doubt over some which appear to be unusually narrow. Penhill in Somerset is only 7.3m wide and may be a pillow mound. Crowmarsh, Oxfordshire is 10m, Bradford Peverell, West Dorset 11m. However, in contrast, at 101m in length by 28m width, Trainford Brow in Cumbria equates in size to some of the southern long barrows such as Old Ditch, Tilshead, and West Kennet, both in Wiltshire, or East Heslerton and Charleston Farm (*colour*

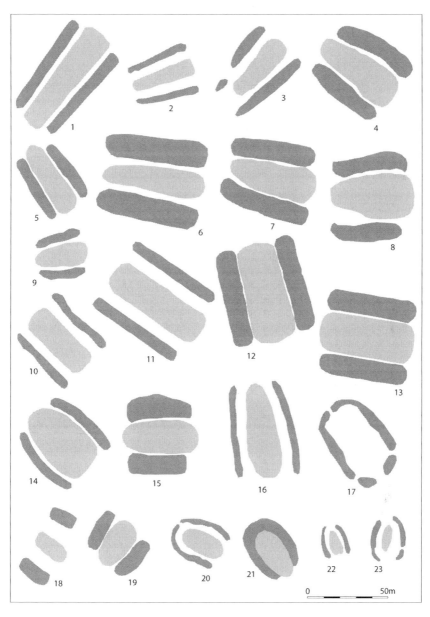

8 Outline plans of long barrows for comparison with north to top. 1. Whitchurch, Hampshire; 2. Fussell's Lodge, Wiltshire; 3. Beckhampton Road, Wiltshire; 4. East Down, Wiltshire; 5. Alton Down, Wiltshire; 6 Danebury West, Nether Wallop, Hampshire; 7. Norton Bavant, Wiltshire; 8. Ell Barrow, Wiltshire; 9. Moody's Down West, Hampshire; 10. South Street, Wiltshire; 11. Wonston, Hampshire; 12. Rockbourne, Hampshire; 13. Danebury East, Nether Wallop, Hampshire; 14. Moody's Down South-East, Hampshire; 15. Boles barrow; 16. Grans Barrow, Rockbourne, Hampshire; 17. Wor Barrow, Dorset; 18. Imber Down; 19. Knook; 20. Thickthorn Down, Dorset; 21. Whitsbury Down, Hampshire; 22. Wayland's Smithy 1, Oxfordshire; 23. Alfriston, East Sussex *plate 3*) in Yorkshire. Only Maiden Castle at 546m, Long Bredy at 195m (*9* and *colour plate 4*) and Broadmayne, at 180m in length, all in Dorset, stand out as significantly different from the longest long barrows and it is these that must provide the yardstick. However, changes in alignment at both Maiden Castle and Long Bredy indicate that their length may in fact be a result of conjoining separate monuments (Bradley 1983). Examples in Dorset were first brought to attention by O.G.S. Crawford (1938) after Mortimer Wheeler's excavation at Maiden Castle. Here it was clear that the barrow was constructed over the silted up ditch of a causewayed enclosure. The relationship implies that in its developed form this bank barrow, at least, would appear to date to after the main period of long barrow use.

There are currently about 140 cursus monuments known in the UK and the numbers increase annually as aerial surveys, in particular, the National Mapping Programme progress. Only parts of the Dorset, Stonehenge and one of the Rudston examples survive as earthworks (*10*), but it is with the plough-levelled examples that distinctions become confusing. Like long barrows, cursus monuments are characterised by parallel ditches, but they are generally further apart and in length extend over much greater distances. The National Mapping

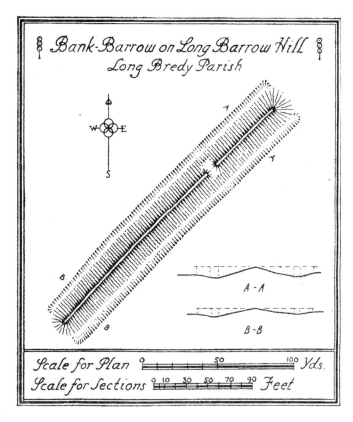

9 Plan of Long Bredy Bank Barrow. *Crown copyright NMR*

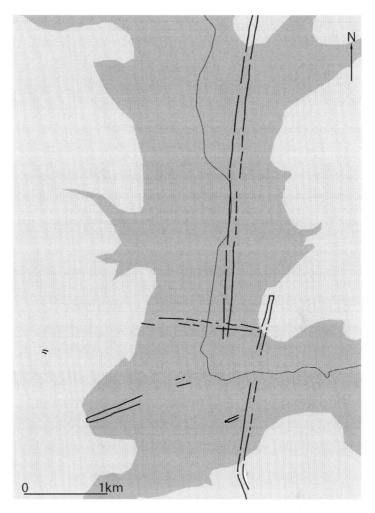

10 Rudston, Yorkshire, redrawn from the air survey plot by Cathy Stoertz (RCHME 1997) showing four cursus monuments that focus on the Gypsy Race stream. A long mortuary enclosure or bank barrow, much narrower than the cursus, lies towards the south and note in particular the round barrow at its west end, while the twin ditches of a long barrow are situated on the valley slopes in the west

Programme defines them as over 250m in length, with the length to width ratio of 10:1, although this presumes that a considerable length can be observed. Where complete, the cursus monuments end in squared or rounded terminals. The few extant cursus monuments make it clear that the spoil from the ditch was placed alongside as a bank, although at some excavated sites, for example, Stanwell, Scorton, and the Cleaven Dyke it is placed centrally.

Thus variation is immense and scope for misinterpretation considerable. Nevertheless a number of threads, themes and architectural preferences provide some persuasion that long barrows as a type are distinct. To investigate further and unravel the data it is necessary now to consider the way in which ideas concerning function developed, as ever more sites were investigated.

2

BATTLE BARROWS AND CLEFT SKULLS

THE IDEA OF FUNERARY MOUNDS

Early in the spring of 1702, Hineage Finch left Wye Court in Kent and made his way the 6km alongside the River Stour to Chilham, where a large mound was situated at the base of the slope on a low bluff just above the floodplain of the river. Unusually, it was oriented across the contours and faced downhill in a northerly direction. At the request of his friend and relative Thomas Thynne, he sunk a small shaft into it and, perhaps assured in the optimism accompanying the coronation of Queen Anne that year and comfortable in the buoyant economy of the early years of the eighteenth century, they both hoped for positive results, along with confirmation of their theories. Both men were well grounded in history and intrigued by antiquarian enquiry and were familiar with the comment made by William Camden in his *Britannia* that the mound might be the burial place of Laberius Durus, a Tribune killed by the British in 54 BC after a battle that took place nearby. At 1.5m, the shaft was just wide enough for one individual and it is likely that both Finch and Thynne sat in supervision, while a third person laboured. From this shaft, a trench of similar width was taken along the summit of the mound for almost 5m. The matrix was found to be loose broken chalk, but at a depth of 1.5m a deposit of soft, damp, dark material some 0.5m thick, was found to contain a few fragments of bones and teeth that crumbled to dust when touched and in some cases it was found to be difficult to determine whether they were animal or human. There were certainly fowl or rabbit-sized bones and some fragments of antler and, given the presence of animal remains, Finch found it difficult to reconcile the idea of the mound as a Roman grave, unless, he thought, they were remnants of sacrifices. Finch (1647-1719) of Winchelsea was later to become First Earl of Aylesford, while Thynne,

Lord Weymouth lived at Longleat in Wiltshire and will have been very familiar with the many tumuli, or earthen mounds, on Salisbury Plain. Both worked in Queen Anne's government, but however the partnership began, the intervention signalled the beginning of an increasing curiosity with the contents of the mysterious earthen mounds that punctuated the British countryside. It may have been around the same time that a long mound at Chettle, in Dorset (*colour plate 5*) 'had an opening made in its side by the Countess of Temple when, beneath the level of the surface of the field, a great quantity of human bones were found, and with them heads of spears and other warlike instruments'. The finds were presented to the Earl of Pembroke, and incorporated into his collection of antiquities at Wilton House, near Salisbury.

There may have been a long-standing rivalry between the owners of these two large neighbouring country estates in Wiltshire. In his *Brief Lives*, Aubrey commented on how in the early seventeenth century, Wilton House was like a college or academy, a meeting place for those studying science and natural history. Defoe visited in the early eighteenth century during his travels through Britain and referred to the house as a museum and Lord Pembroke, its owner, as a collector of antiquities. Having observed the great number of barrows on the downs, he commented that 'the Barrows, as we all agree to call them, are very many in number in this county, and very obvious, having suffered little decay. These are large hillocks of earth cast up, as the antients agree, by the soldiers over the bodies of their dead comrades slain in battle; several hundreds of these are to be seen...' (Defoe 1724, 201).

Lord Pembroke appears to have enlarged his collection by digging into the local barrows and his excavations into mounds near Stonehenge also influenced William Stukeley. Having assisted in the excavations, Stukeley was encouraged to investigate others and he cut into several round barrows before turning his attention to a small and shallow, but long, mound on Normanton Down situated east of the track to Wilton, south of Stonehenge. In it he made 'at the north end a long cutt 28 feet (8.5m) north and south five foot (1.5m) broad we dug down to the solid chalk and found nothing' (Burl and Mortimer 2005, 103). This is almost certainly Wilsford South 13, a small, undistinguished mound close to the better known Bush Barrow (*11*) and although dwarfed by some of the Bronze Age mounds, set neatly among the Normanton barrow group. Stukeley described it as small, giving its length as 60 Celtic feet and width as 30 Celtic feet. Assuming that these measurements were similar to modern imperial 'feet', it converts to 18.2 x 9.1m, which is close to the dimensions given by the Ordnance Survey Archaeological Division for this mound.

Attempting to classify the mounds, Stukeley thought the disc barrows were aesthetically perfect and must therefore be the burial places of druids.

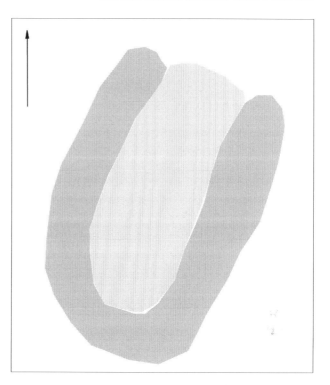

11 Outline plan of long barrow on Normanton Down, Wiltshire with a U-shaped ditch reminiscent of some in Cranborne Chase. This was the first such mound known to be excavated in Wessex when William Stukeley placed a trench in the north end of it in the eighteenth century, but although digging down to the underlying chalk he found nothing. The mound was subsequently dwarfed by a large round barrow and overshadowed by the 'Bush Barrow' just 200m to the south-west

Subsequently, having been told that a 'brass celt' had been found in a long barrow, 'farthest north from Stonehenge' and presumably therefore either Figheldean, Durrington Down or Knighton long barrow, he considered that the longer mounds must be the burial places of archdruids (Burl and Mortimer 2005, 29). Stukeley (1743, 45) also described the long barrows in the Avebury area:

> There are likewise about Abury some pyriform barrows, longish but broad at one end: some composed of earth, thrown into a tumulus. Of this sort a very long one in the valley from Bekamton to Runway-hill. Another among the furze bushes south of Silbury, set with stones, which farmer Green carried away. Others made of stones set upright in that form. Of the latter, a very large one in Monkton-fields, about 20 stones left on one side is directly north of Abury town. Another such south of Silbury-hill. Another pyriform, made only of earth, under Runway-hill. Another on the hill south-west from Bekamton, cut through with some later division dike.

The latter can only have been the bell barrow on Horton Down, which has an early medieval estate or parish boundary cut across it and the mistake concerning the type of mound indicates that Stukeley, writing some years later, relied on a sometimes fading memory. His reference to a 'very long one' in the Beckhampton to Roundway valley is intriguing. There appears to be no illustration of this and it presumably refers to the Beckhampton Road barrow excavated by Isobel Smith in 1964, which then survived to a by no means excessive length of less than 50m.

Stukeley hailed from Lincolnshire and despite travelling widely within Britain, his comments were largely restricted to the barrows around Stonehenge and Avebury. He mentioned in passing 'a large long barrow' on Portsdown, overlooking the coastal plain at Portsmouth, which must surely be that known as Bevis' Grave, now sadly destroyed. He also made a number of sketches of Jullieberrie's Grave, showing it as angled down slope and with a bulbous feature on a slightly different alignment at its head, introducing the possibility that there were formerly two mounds. He mentioned another mound, 'a vast barrow' 106m by 36m wide, not recorded in the archive, at Cossington, near Leicester (Stukeley 1776) which, oriented north to south, lay close to the River Wrenkin and occupied a similar landscape position to Jullieberrie's Grave.

The second edition of a new archaeological journal, *Archaeologia*, published in 1773, carried articles on the enormous mound at New Grange in Ireland as well as the excavation of a large barrow at Ellenborough in Cumberland (Head 1773). It also focused attention on the rich burials found in some of the mounds on the steppes of Russia, in particular, the enormous mound at Tomsky with its extravagantly rich burials which may have inspired the excavation of Silbury Hill by the Duke of Northumberland and Colonel Drax in 1776. This might have been expected to have tremendous impact on the investigation of barrows in Britain, but the lack of rich graves at Silbury, coupled with the pre-occupation over the war with America, may have affected matters. Certainly there was little recorded activity until the turn of the century. The Reverend Pegg's investigation of barrows in Derbyshire highlighted, but no more, that long barrows were present in the British landscape, '… of an oblong form, as what is called Julabert's Grave at Chilham in Kent, and another large barrow on Wye Downs, which though upon a much larger scale, are not unlike our common graves' (Pegg 1785).

The work of two individuals, both based in Wiltshire, provided the study of long barrows with a firm foundation and sound history during the nineteenth century. While William Cunnington, a draper and cloth merchant of Heytesbury, was concerned with internal structures and function, John Thurnam, Medical Superintendent of the County Lunatic Asylum at Devizes, was more impressed with the burials and artefacts and, in particular, placed special emphasis on the skulls. To some extent there was replication, but to a great extent the studies complemented each other.

Investigations by William Cunnington, represented a major advance. Diagnosed of poor health and instructed by his doctor to spend more time in the fresh air, he took to investigating the mounds on the nearby downs with considerable enthusiasm (R.H. Cunnington 1975). There was no guide or template to follow, apart from some published diggings into early medieval mounds by the Reverend Douglas in Kent and if there had been other earlier investigations they remained unrecorded. Having dug into the long mound situated on the edge of Heytesbury North Field in 1800, Cunnington went on to excavate seventeen others during the next eight years, re-visiting several in order to clarify points as new questions arose and his knowledge of the subject developed. His early efforts were financially supported by the local MP, H.P. Wyndham, who was interested in the theory that these mounds covered individuals killed in ancient battles. Later, Richard (Colt) Hoare of Stourhead replaced him as benefactor and, using the data from Cunnington's excavations, prepared the first volume of *Ancient Wiltshire*, which was originally published in fascicules between 1810 and 1812. As part of this work Hoare employed the surveyor Philip Crocker, who at the time was engaged on work for the Ordnance Survey in preparation of the 1st edition map of Wiltshire, thus ensuring that archaeology, including many barrows, appeared on the map. No accurate map of the downs formerly existed, nor was there any antiquarian forerunner of the Sites and Monuments Record and the location of most were recorded for the first time.

Cunnington appears to have made daily notes, but unfortunately they only survive for part of the excavation of King Barrow in 1800, although reports were made to Wyndham and subsequently Hoare of the results of his other explorations in the form of a series of letters, copied out by his daughters (Eagles and Field 2004). They include basic descriptions of each mound and details of the stratigraphy and features encountered, comments on finds of human and animal bones and other artefacts and very occasionally a sketch plan. Sequence within the deposits was an important factor, as he was acutely aware of the relative chronology of primary and secondary burials and he discerned a difference between the skeletons found in the upper layers of the barrows, which were often accompanied by swords or other metal objects and those skeletons found on or close to the old ground surface without accoutrements. Having visited Cunnington's excavations at Sherrington long barrow, and witnessed the presence of burials with iron grave goods, Wyndham considered the mound to be Saxon, but Cunnington, along with the excavators Stephen and John Parker, protested and expressed the view that the Saxon material was merely secondary (*12*).

In contrast to Stukeley's views, Wyndham reasoned that as the round mounds around Stonehenge covered single skeletons, the long mounds must be the burial place of a number of individuals. It thus followed that they must cover those

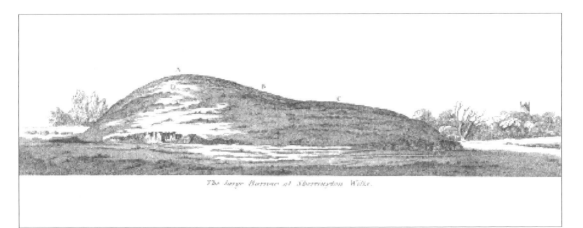

12 The long barrow at Sherrington, Wiltshire as drawn by Philip Crocker (original in Lambert 1806). The gravel constructed mound is situated on the bank of the River Wylye, but has since been drastically curtailed. Amongst charred wood and ashes at the base of the mound Cunnington, who excavated it in 1804 found a skeleton of a pig and a large unidentified bird. Within a neatly cut pit was a cattle skull and a deer antler

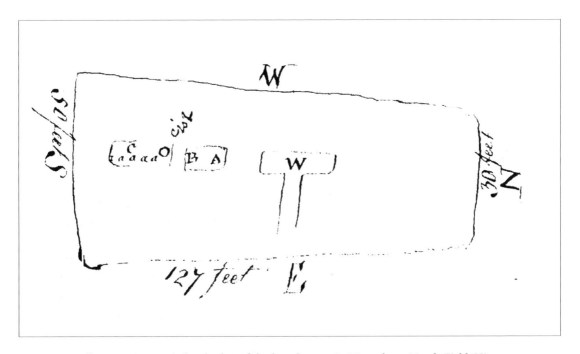

13 William Cunnington's sketch plan of the long barrow in Heytesbury North Field. His trenches encountered a circular mound at the east end composed of black earth mixed with sarsens, flint nodules and chalk, beneath which was a circular pit cut into the chalk adjacent to which lay a great number of human bones representing as many as 20 individuals. *Courtesy of the Wiltshire Heritage Museum*

vanquished in battle and he termed them Battle Barrows. Cunnington was more open minded and cautious. He acknowledged that in some cases, particularly at Boles Barrow, there were large numbers of skeletons, but he considered it unlikely for stone pavements to be constructed, or cairns of large stones erected for the burial of an enemy by the victor. Equally he questioned why such an enormous amount of earth as that at Old Ditch long barrow should be erected over just three persons or at Knook over four. He was equally perplexed about the considerable numbers of animal bones that appeared to receive the same treatment as human bones in, for example, King Barrow. Cunnington also concluded that 'everything that we see in these long barrows militates against the suggestion of their being family sepulchres'. Nevertheless, numbers of skeletons were found and the natural assumption by others was that the covering mound formed their burial place and monument.

The first mound investigated was just over a kilometre from Cunnington's home at Heytesbury, on the edge of the downland in Heytesbury North Field. He targeted the centre of the mound expecting it, not unreasonably, to have been the focal point. He cut a trench 5m long and *c*.2.5m wide and, at the base of the mound encountered a deposit of 'black earth', something that in due course was to intrigue both Cunnington and Wyndham, as similar deposits were encountered elsewhere (*13*). At Tilshead Old Ditch long barrow, he recorded a deposit of black earth laid along the length of the barrow and there was a similar layer at Knook. Concerned by this, Hoare consulted chemists Mr Hatchett and Dr Gibbs, who both indicated that it was not the result of fire and as the analysis failed to detect 'animal matter', Hoare subsequently concluded that it represented decayed turf, and that is probably how it would be interpreted today. However, discussion as to whether it was blood was considerable and the matter was revived when some time later, chemical analysis of the black earth beneath Boles Barrow by Cunnington's grandson (also named William) was found to contain ammonia and it was then concluded that the material must indeed be blood (Cunnington 1889).

Soon after his initial exploration, Cunnington set his sights on the enormous mound known as King Barrow, at Boreham, near Warminster, just a few kilometres further along the River Wylye (*14*). At 62m in length and 17m in width, this is one of the largest mounds on Salisbury Plain. It still survives to a massive 4.5m high and its position on the edge of a bluff gives it the impression of even greater height when viewed from the valley floor. As at Heytesbury, Cunnington initially opened a trench towards the centre, before turning along the axis of the mound in either direction, leaving a T-shaped cutting. The mound comprised a covering of white chalk, beneath which was a matrix of 'white Marley Earth' supplemented by 'vegetable mould' with nodules of pyrites.

At the base was a floor of yellow clay, almost 1m lower than the surrounding ground surface and which appeared to extend beyond the edge of the covering mound. It was stained a dull red 'as blood appears on the roads a few days after it has been shed' and covered with animal bones 'both beasts and birds', as well as pieces of antler, some fragments of human bones, charred wood, and pottery. The description suggests that prior to construction of the mound, a platform may have been levelled into the side of the slope, the yellowed clay perhaps representing weathered and trampled chalk, on which activities including the making and use of fires, perhaps cremation pyres, took place.

The following year he investigated Boles Barrow (Cunnington referred to it as Boles – later writers using Bowl's instead) and provided Wyndham with the kind of information that unfortunately only encouraged his views. Beneath a white chalk covering, at a depth of 1.4m, the top of a cairn 'in form like the ridge of a house' became visible, comprising large stones of sarsen and flint and set lengthways for two-thirds of the mound, becoming wider towards the base. The cairn was almost 2m high and beneath it was a well-laid pavement of flint nodules on which were laid a large number of 'human bodies, but placed in no regular order'. Adjacent to these, a pit that Cunnington referred to as a cist, was found neatly cut into the chalk. He thought that it was similar to those found under some round barrows and in which burials had been found, although there was no such burial in this. Unfortunately, he felt unable to satisfactorily investigate further as a result of unstable boulders falling from the cairn (15). The sequence of black earth – pit (cist) – pavement – cairn or mound – followed by barrow construction was subsequently encountered at other mounds.

In 1802, Cunnington turned his attention to the long barrows around Tilshead. Five such mounds are situated on the downs above the village and he dug into three of them. The first, the largest long barrow in Wiltshire, lay alongside an old boundary ditch, now known to be Bronze Age in date, and because of this it has become known as 'Old Ditch' long barrow (*colour plate 6*). The mound is enormous, twice the length of most long barrows in Wiltshire, and unfortunately the detail of Cunnington's investigation is a little unclear as his description refers to, and depends upon, a now lost plan. Instead of trenching in from the side, he appears to have placed a considerable cutting at least 10m in length along the summit, finishing 26m from the east end. At the base was the usual deposit of black sooty earth, here ridged almost to 0.5m in height, but decreasing towards the edges and thought by Cunnington to perhaps extend for the whole length of the barrow. At one point, where much charred wood and fragments of antler were discovered, the trench was extended to north, south and west. The black earth appeared to rise in height and 'different strata' gave it the appearance of a circular barrow that he considered had existed prior to the construction of the

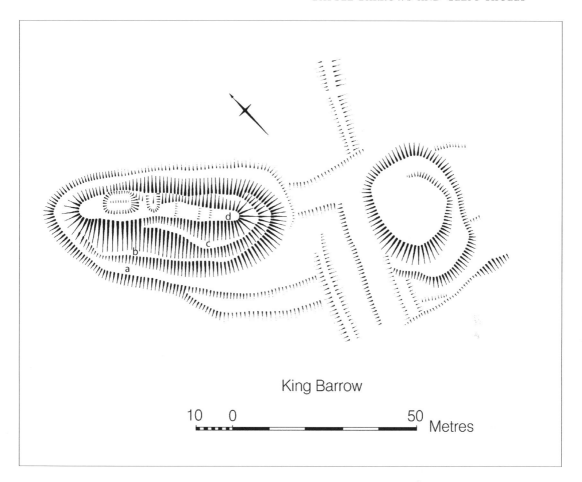

14 Earthwork plan of King Barrow, Boreham, near Warminster. When Cunnington excavated here in 1800 and again in 1809 he encountered a floor of yellow clay which was in places stained a dull red and covered with animal bones ashes and charred wood. It extended for a considerable distance beyond the confines of the barrow. On this and merging with it was a round mound of clay just under 1m in height and a little over 3m in diameter within which were more animal bones as well as several burnt human bones. Animals and humans it appears had received similar treatment. The round mound to the south-east has been landscaped and incorporated into a garden layout. © *Crown copyright NMR*

long mound. Finding no evidence of battle victims he moved on to investigate the west end, where he cut a considerable section and encountered a pavement of flints similar to that found at Boles Barrow. Here, three human skeletons lay. Cunnington extended the trench but found the deposits confined to the pavement, and encountered nothing further east but the sooty black earth. In contrast to Boles Barrow, the pavement contained an 'immense quantity of ashes and charred wood' as well as several large bones thought to be human that were

15 Bluestone formerly thought to have been found in Bolesbarrow but recent analysis suggests that it may have come from Stonehenge. *Courtesy of the Salisbury and South Wiltshire Museum*

partly burnt. The burial deposit was evidently more complex. He wondered why such a large mound of earth was constructed just for the burial of three people when the lack of grave goods implied that they were of no special social standing.

From early in his campaign, it is clear that Cunnington was aware of potential differences in the form of the mound, both Tilshead Lodge long barrow and White Barrow (*colour plate 7*) were wedge-shaped and he, in contrast, described Boles Barrow and Sherrington long barrows as like 'an egg cut in two lengthways', with the convex side placed uppermost. Hoare used his words almost verbatim, and went on 'some are almost of a triangular form; whilst others are thrown up in a long ridge of a nearly equal breadth at each end; but we find generally one end of these barrows broader than the other, and that broad end pointing towards the east' (*16*).

By the end of 1802 it was clear that skeletal material lay at the easternmost or largest end of the barrows rather than in the centre and in a second phase of work Cunnington began to re-visit some of the mounds to check this observation. He reinvestigated Corton, by cutting a trench at the east end and encountered two pits at the base of the mound, each over 1m in diameter and *c.*0.7m deep, both were neatly cut into the underlying chalk and between them lay eight human skeletons arranged in no particular order and in different directions. He also returned to the mound in Heytesbury North Field early in 1804 and placed two further trenches at the broad end, the position marked on a sketch plan of the barrow is the earliest excavation drawing of a Neolithic site (*13*). The 'black earth' was observed to increase in height towards the second trench and, mixed with sarsens, flint nodules and chalk marl rose to form what appeared to be a circular barrow similar to that encountered at Old Ditch.

Like Hineage Finch before him during the investigation at Jullieberrie's Grave, Cunnington continued to be intrigued by the large number of animal bones often found together with human remains and, in 1809, following the digging for chalk in King Barrow by the landowner, Mr Morgan, he utilised the diggings in a further investigation. Unfortunately, although adding detail to his earlier work, the results were very similar and simply served to confirm his earlier findings.

As Hoare replaced Wyndham as benefactor, Cunnington deferred to Hoare's wider knowledge concerning antiquities and his notes became less descriptive. Nevertheless, together they excavated a number of other long barrows, in particular, those within about 2km of Stonehenge, Amesbury 10a, Amesbury 14, Durrington 63, Wilsford 30 and Winterbourne Stoke 53; the results all being recounted in *Ancient Wiltshire*, until Cunnington's death in 1810, after which Hoare's investigations into long barrows were largely brought to a halt.

16 Richard Hoare brought together
Cunnington's work in his *Ancient Wiltshire*
the first fascicule of which was published
in 1810. Hoare produced a typology of all
barrows based on the plan and profile of
the mounds and ditches amongst which he
identified two types of long barrow

The opening of barrows continued as a gentlemanly pastime. Pistledown,
Dorset, was opened in 1828 and found to be composed of 'gravely soil'.
Excavations to a depth of 1.5m were considered unsuccessful as no interment
was discovered, although four leaf- (lozenge-) shaped arrowheads were recovered
(Warne 1866, 5, 16). No such artefacts had been discovered by Cunnington
during his investigations but the four arrowheads could later be compared to
the four found in a round mound overlying a long barrow on Seamer Moor,
Yorkshire and opened by Lord A.D. Conyngham (Conyngham 1849) and which
became well-known as part of the Seamer axe hoard.

Despite such interventions it was almost 50 years after Cunnington's death
before John Thurnam's comprehensive and effective investigation into barrows
and their contents and which, in turn, was so influential to Stuart Piggott's work
and description of the Windmill Hill and Wessex cultures. Thurnam, a Member
of the Royal College of Surgeons with an interest in skull capacity and shape,
moved to Wiltshire in 1851. Having published articles on barrows and their
contents at Lamel Hill, York and in Denmark in 1849 and 1850, and as one of the
founding officers of the Wiltshire Archaeological and Natural History Society
(Piggott 1991, 111), he quickly realised that the barrows on the local downs
provided an ideal opportunity for studying early skeletal material. Using his
patients as labour force, he dug into a number of mounds (Piggott 1993, 3): West
Kennet in 1859, Norton Bavant in 1863. Unlike Cunnington, however, he rarely
described the excavation itself, or the deposits encountered and seems to have
left no plans or section drawings. At Figheldean, for example, we merely learn
that 'there was great trouble in finding the interment in this mound, it being
exceptionally remote from the eastern end' (Thurnam 1869, 184) and are left to
presume that he had trenched much of the eastern half of the barrow during his
exploration.

Thurnam tabulated the data from the *Ancient Wiltshire* study, inspected at first
hand Hoare's collection of material then still at Stourhead (now at Devizes
Museum) and initiated his own research programme (Thurnam 1869), digging
into 22 Wiltshire long barrows between 1855 and 1867, including 6 of those
previously opened by Cunnington.

Thurnam's experience largely confirmed the salient features recorded in Cunnington's excavations. Of the sample then available (31 excavated long barrows), primary burials had been located with greater or lesser certainty in 22. There were rather ambiguous results from eight others and no evidence at all from three. Of the 22, all but one consisted of one or more skeletons placed on or close to the old ground surface at the broader end, generally the easternmost. Eight had pits cut into the chalk, and he noted that in all probability they existed in other barrows but had simply been unlocated by the excavation. In one case, a skeleton was found in a pit and in another a cattle skull and piece of antler. Hoare had considered that the pits may have been for 'some particular ceremony' and Thurnam supported this view using classical and ethnographic examples to suggest that they were for pouring the blood of sacrifices into, or for offerings of food for the dead (Thurnam 1869, 141). Having excavated the mound at West Kennet and encountered a stone chamber, he ignored Hoare's subdivision based on mounds and ditches and, in the first of two influential articles (1869 and 1871), divided them principally into chambered and unchambered types.

Meanwhile, Thurnam's contemporary, William Greenwell, a canon of Durham Cathedral, was excavating mounds in the north of the country. He had worked with Thurnam in Wiltshire in 1863, probably at West Kennet and Winterbourne Stoke as his collection contained material from those sites (Kinnes and Longworth 1985, 141) and during the years following his visit to Wiltshire went on to excavate 10 long and 6 oval barrows in Yorkshire.

The first was Ebberston, opened in 1864. He reported it as being composed of oolite rubble mixed with clay. Given his experiences in Wiltshire, he must have anticipated the recovery of no burials at the west end of the mound, yet cut a trench at that point, which encountered a wall of limestone flagstones embedded in clay. He then reopened the scar of a former trench 6m from the east end and as it was explored to the 'east we came upon the signs of burning, at first slight but gradually becoming more evident, in burnt earth, stones and bones, together with charcoal until at the east end the oolitic limestone became lime, and all traces of bone had disappeared.' Towards the west end was a stone cairn 5.5m in diameter and regularly constructed with ' ... stones carefully laid in order from a central point ... nothing was seen when the pile was removed but the layer of forced clay before mentioned' (Greenwell 1865, 103-5). Similar features were subsequently encountered in Westow and Crosby Garrett long barrows. For the first time a clue presented itself as to the processes involved that had so intrigued Cunnington at King's Barrow in Wiltshire. Greenwell explained the mound as forming a kind of kiln, with stones arranged along the axis of the barrow to create a flue in order to make a draught. At the east end was burnt clay and stones, while the oolitic limestone had turned to lime and all trace of bone incinerated. To the east of the cairn, lying in yellow clay were the remains of at least 14 bodies described in similar terms to those of Cunnington at Boles Barrow, 'not laid in any order, but with the component bones broken scattered and lying in the most confused manner … half a jaw for instance upon part of a thigh bone'. He was certain that this was not a result of later disturbance but that they had been originally deposited in that manner and he concluded that they must have had the flesh removed before being placed on the floor.

At Westow, a barrow on the valley slope of the River Derwent, primary burials lying on a pavement of flagstones occupied a space about 1.4m wide and situated for 9m along an axial line at the eastern end of the mound. Adjacent to them was a 2m wide trench, cut for 0.3m into the bedrock, with slabs of oolitic limestone at each end with a third between them forming two compartments. These were filled with burnt earth, but no bones. Above both trench and burial pavement was a low ridged cairn 1.4m wide, which rose to the surface of the mound. Again the description is familiar.

Canon Greenwell had worked with Colonel Augustus Lane-Fox during the latter part of his excavations at Cissbury in 1868 and there is some indication that Greenwell might have considered Lane-Fox a 'pupil', but there was evidently a difference of opinion concerning interpretation of the site at Cissbury, perhaps resulting from envy of Lane-Fox's careful excavation technique. The nature of this can be gauged from the section drawings and photographs at Cissbury which, even then was far superior to the techniques used by Greenwell. Whereas, like Cunnington before him, Lane-Fox strove to understand the nature and development of the deposits on site, Greenwell's knowledge of prehistory was understood primarily through artefacts. Nevertheless, Greenwell's influence was considerable. In excavating barrows he initially cut a series of trenches across the entire central part of the mound, his workforce advancing in a line (Kinnes and Longworth 1985) and the technique was subsequently adopted by his 'pupil' at Wor Barrow.

On inheriting the Rushmore estate in Dorset after adopting the name of Pitt Rivers, Lane-Fox set about excavating sites on Cranbourne Chase and in 1893 turned his attention to a long oval mound, Wor Barrow situated on Handley Down, adjacent to a complex of round mounds interrupted in turn by a Roman Road and known as the Oakley Down cemetery. Having unsuccessfully searched the ground to both west and south-west of the mound for subtle surface earthworks that might betray the presence of settlement, he went on the explore the area by percussion, using a pick to hammer on the surface and note the change in sound. The Angle Ditch, a Bronze Age settlement site was discovered just 50m away from the barrow as a result. The technique, called 'bosing', was re-established by the Curwens in Sussex during the 1920s. It may have been Toms,

Pitt Rivers former surveyor, who introduced them to the method as he had moved to Sussex and was responsible for surveying a number of long mounds there (*17*). Compared to his contemporaries Pitt Rivers was methodical. Before excavating, a careful survey of the mound was made and the contours plotted. He was aware that by excavating the site would be destroyed and that it was important to have an adequate record. He first emptied the side ditches, carefully recording the sequence of deposits as well as the position and level of any finds in them. He subsequently cut a 14m wide trench longitudinally from south to north through the centre of the barrow leaving four central pillars standing in order to assist with interpretation. Beginning in the south and first removing surface materials to encounter any secondary burials he then took the trench down to and below the old ground surface.

In general, the results confirmed those of Cunnington, though provided much greater detail. Six primary interments were placed together in a small space, with a small oval pit on either side of them and all covered by a round mound of turf. However, this was located towards the eastern end of a rectangular enclosure defined by a bedding trench that had once held posts. The round mound lay within what Richard Atkinson later considered to be a long mortuary enclosure (Atkinson 1951). Two Neolithic skeletons lay in the long barrow ditch and above them and in the upper levels of the mound were a series of secondary burials associated with Romano-British pottery.

The spoil from the barrow was placed outside the ditch and formed into a terraced arena (Pitt Rivers 1898, 74). Pitt Rivers had created the Larmer Tree pleasure grounds in order to encourage visitors to enjoy the estate and the intention was to use the excavated barrow as an amphitheatre for games and amusements, a kind of parkland folly. However, it does not appear to have been so used and it remains in the same condition today (Bowden 1991).

Concern at the sheer number of monuments being threatened by cultivation in the early years of the twentieth century led to the establishment of an Earthworks Committee by the Congress of Archaeological Societies and there was encouragement to record as much as possible before it disappeared. The Rev. E.A. Downman, from Laindon in Essex, recorded and surveyed large numbers of sites of all kinds for the early volumes of the Victoria County History, while Hadrian Allcroft (1908) and Heywood Sumner (1913) produced volumes of earthwork studies. Already by the turn of the century the Ordnance Survey were incorporating archaeological sites on their maps as a matter of course and it was to be the Ordnance Survey Archaeology Division that became the major player in archaeological fieldwork during the early part of the twentieth century.

While a considerable body of evidence had been assembled, the results of the careful excavation techniques used by Pitt Rivers at Wor Barrow posed further

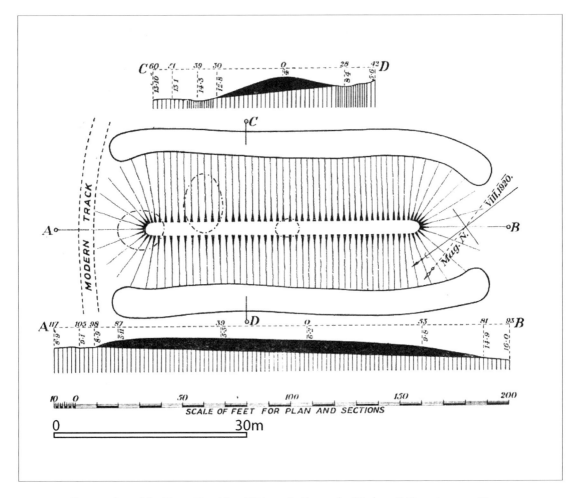

17 Survey plan of the 'Long Burgh' at Alfriston in Sussex by Herbert S. Toms in 1920. *From Toms 1922*

questions that could not easily be answered. In July and August of 1914, O.G.S. Crawford assisted by Dr E.A. Hooton, a physical anthropologist who had begun teaching at Harvard University the year before, investigated a small long barrow and at least three round barrows situated on the upper slopes alongside a now dry coombe that fed down to join the River Bourne at Collingbourne Ducis, at Wexcombe, near Grafton. The long mound was adjacent to a group of seven round barrows, while at least one further round barrow lay in the bottom below, close to a winterbourne spring (*colour plate 8*). The long mound, referred to as Tow Barrow on Andrews and Dury's Map of Wiltshire of 1773, was no more than 27.5m in length and little more than 1.5m in height. Unfortunately, the first 'scientific' excavation into a long barrow in the twentieth century was interrupted by the outbreak of the First World War. This curtailed activities and Hooton evidently returned to Harvard in the US, perhaps with the site archive; consequently little was published and the site was unfortunately largely forgotten. However, the excavation notes were later seen by Col C.D. Drew and Stuart Piggott (1936) who observed that there were no indications of the presence of timber, but there were irregular heaps of turf resembling those at Thickthorn Down long barrow in Dorset, which they had recently been engaged in excavating. Fragments of bones of three individuals, said to represent the primary interment, were found in the mound but nothing further is known about them and enquiries in Britain and in the US failed to trace them or the site archive. According to Drew and Piggott (1936), the bones were evidently deliberately broken and scattered on the old ground surface at the east end of the mound. Ten sherds of Neolithic pottery found within a deposit of black soil marking the old ground surface were returned to Devizes Museum in 1940. They were found close to the southern end of the mound within a small area of between two and three square metres (Anon 1920, 90-1: Crawford 1922, 57: Cunnington M 1940, 164-5). All but one of them could be from the same pot, a bowl with simple rim, dark brown exterior and brown interior and calcined flint temper, but they do not form a complete pot. Either portions of it had been removed in antiquity or the vessel had been broken elsewhere and only fragments placed at the site.

THE 1930S

In preparing an inventory and map of long barrows in Wessex for the Ordnance Survey, Crawford considered that most long barrows were of earth, stone chambers occurring only when barrows were built in areas that possessed usable stone. Taking the evidence of the stone chamber from West Kennet into account, it was thought that the earthen long barrows also contained burial chambers, but constructed of wood instead of stone and, in preparing the inventory, it was considered that 'any subdivision into chambered and unchambered types is meaningless' (Ordnance Survey 1932).

Crawford's successor at the Ordnance Survey, C.W. Phillips, pursued the matter across eastern England in 1929, recording the presence of a newly discovered group of 11 or possibly 12 mounds in Lincolnshire during archaeological fieldwork for the revision of the Ordnance Survey 6in map. He distinguished them from the Cotswold examples that had been identified by Crawford, as the latter had walled features that projected, horn-like, from each side at the larger end, forming a partially enclosed forecourt and, from the Wessex monuments by the lack of side ditches. However, indications of collapsed material towards the easternmost end suggested that some may have contained wooden chambers. He excavated at Skendleby (Phillips 1936) and supplemented this with partial excavation of a second at Therfield Heath, Royston, Hertfordshire (Phillips 1935), but the results were rather more complex than expected and involved possible structures of turf and components formed by fences.

Thurnam's classification, however, was supported by Stuart Piggott, who accepted the 'chambered' and 'unchambered' division, although substituted the term 'earthen' for the latter (Piggott 1935). Piggott (1935) considered that the 'chambered' or megalithic examples were more angular, being straight sided and of wedge-shaped plan, in contrast to the less angular earthen examples. His distribution map demonstrated that the greatest accumulation of long barrows of all types was in Wessex, with lesser clusters in Yorkshire and Lincolnshire and only isolated examples elsewhere. In large parts of the country there was a complete absence. Chambered barrows predominated in the west and north where suitable stone existed, while those without chambers were distributed in the south and east, but principally around Salisbury Plain and in Dorset. Wessex, therefore, was considered to have played a primary role in the dissemination of cultural ideas and he preferred the notion of influences radiating from Salisbury Plain to the stone using areas rather than the other way around. While he acknowledged Mrs Maud Cunnington's important observation that in the area around Avebury, an area that contained plentiful sarsen, not all of the barrows were megalithic (Cunnington 1934, 74), he was dismissive of Crawford's view repeated in *Wessex from the Air* (Crawford and Keiller 1929) that earthen barrows were simply a version of megalithic monuments situated in areas lacking stone. He also ignored the point made by Pitt Rivers 40 years earlier that wooden chambers may exist beneath some mounds (Pitt Rivers 1898 preface). He did acknowledge, however, that in the west of England, where geology assured the availability of suitable stone, the mounds themselves could be built of stone instead of 'earth' (*colour plate 9*).

Until then, typological division had been based on the simple existence of a stone chamber within the mound, but Piggott's criteria introduced the construction material of the mound itself. One problem here was that without excavation, not only was it impossible to tell whether there was either a chamber within, but it was usually difficult to determine whether the mound itself, invariably turf covered, was really a cairn. Only the presence of a slightly greater density of stone at Old Wingate, Durham, indicates that the mound could be a cairn (*18*). Further problems occurred in areas such as the North Wiltshire Downs, or Devon, where it was clear that some mounds composed of earth, nevertheless harboured megalithic chambers and these could only be considered

18 Long mound at Old Wingate, Co. Durham. Only a slightly greater surface concentration of stone indicates that the mound may cover a cairn. *Photograph: Pete Topping*

hybrids of the two types. There were other difficulties. At Redhill long barrow in Somerset, for example, a number of large stones were visible but, when visited by an Ordnance Survey Field Investigator, these were considered to have resulted from recent or historic field clearance, being dumped on the mound for agricultural convenience.

Like Cunnington and Thurnam before him, Piggott was aware of the range of forms between, for example, 'such monsters' as Tilshead 'Old Ditch' long barrow, which reaches over 120m in length and much smaller mounds such as Knook Down, a mere 25m. Amongst them a clearly defined local type from the Wiltshire/Dorset border since known as the Cranborne Chase type, in which ditches extend round three sides of the mound. Along with Colonel C.D. Drew, curator of the Dorset county museum, Piggott had completely excavated one of these on Thickthorn Down, Dorset (Piggott and Drew 1936) and found no evidence of either a chamber or a burial and, as they pointed out, the presence of well-preserved animal bones on the uninterrupted old turf line indicated that it was unlikely that any existed. Aside from this, inside just a few years in the 1930s, complete or almost complete excavations of long barrows had occurred at Skendleby 1 (*colour plate 10*), at Holdenhurst, Christchurch, Hampshire (Piggott 1937a), supplemented with partial examination of Therfield Heath, Royston (Phillips 1935), Jullieberrie's Grave, Kent (Jessup 1937; 1939) and Badshot, Farnham, Surrey (Keiller and Piggott 1939). All of this was summed up by J.G.D. Clark in (1937) and it provided a considerable body of new evidence, although still insufficient to allow general conclusions as each new excavation uncovered new and unexpected features. It only served to demonstrate the variety of external form and internal features. Skendleby 1, was rectangular with its ditch, but for a small causeway at the south corner, completely encircling the mound. Within was a rectangular post-built structure with concave façade and with fencing dividing the western end into two, with bays on one side. At Holdenhurst, the ditch was continuous around the widest end. Within it, was a rectangular feature marked out by a turf revetment. At Therfield Heath, an oval mound of turf had a ditch apparently encircling it, while the mound at Badshot Lea, Farnham, Surrey, had been destroyed by quarrying and the site only recognised by its surviving ditches (*19*).

FUSSELL'S LODGE — A NEW FRAMEWORK

Following a hiatus in activity largely due to the interruption of the Second World War, Piggott's views on the Windmill Hill Culture, incorporating causewayed enclosures and earthen, i.e. unchambered long barrows had crystallised considerably and in an influential article he highlighted the possible north European origin of trapezoidal forms (Piggott 1955). A number of rescue investigations were carried out by the Ministry of Works on long barrows at East Heslerton and Seamer Moor in Yorkshire, Nutbane in Hampshire and Woodford in Wiltshire, although apart from Nutbane problems beset their publication. However, the wedge-shaped nature of the mound in Clarendon Park, near Salisbury, that was threatened with cultivation was a perfect site to investigate Piggott's views. Excavated by Paul Ashbee in 1957, work revealed a wooden burial chamber in turn covered by a flint cairn (*22*). Here at last was the wooden equivalent of the stone burial chamber predicted by Crawford, but more besides as the burials were set at the east end of a long trapezoidal mortuary enclosure. The report on Fussell's Lodge long barrow was enormously influential (Ashbee 1966) and remains the most comprehensive analysis of an 'earthen' long barrow in the country; still as relevant as it was 50 years ago.

Atkinson's excavation of a sub-rectangular enclosure at Dorchester in 1948 (Atkinson 1951), a site which lacked a covering mound, allowed immediate comparison with long barrows and the idea was given some support when an extant rectangular enclosure found on Normanton Down, near Stonehenge in 1949 was excavated (*20*). Atkinson perceptively noticed that the Normanton example was similar to that uncovered beneath the long mound at Wor Barrow by Lt General Pitt Rivers (*21*). Increasingly these long enclosure-like forms

19 The mound at Badshot Lea had been quarried away leaving the ditches to be discovered and excavated in 1936. The single post setting at the east end was considered reminiscent of Thickthorn Down long barrow. *Redrawn from Keiller and Piggott 1939*

appear on aerial photographs particularly in the east of the country, often being recorded as cropmarks (Loveday and Petchey 1983).

The rectangular ditched long enclosure at Dorchester, Oxfordshire (Atkinson *et al.* 1951), 61m by 20m, was oriented north-west/south-east and had an internal bank with a human jaw found in it. An entrance gap was placed in the centre of the south-eastern end and there were others through the ditch and bank along each long side. Ebbsfleet pottery was found in a late filling of the ditch, while a cursus ditch with a date from the primary silt of 3510–2920 cal. BC (Whittle *et al.* 1992) cut slightly obliquely through the enclosure effectively putting it out of use. Parallel ditches about 2m apart and subsequently recognised as a trackway associated with a Middle Bronze Age field system also cut across both enclosure and cursus (Bradley and Chambers 1988, 284) and ensured that all trace of the enclosure had been obliterated by the mid-second millennium.

Like many long barrows, the rectangular structure at Normanton was oriented east-north-east with the easternmost end being marginally wider. It was defined by a causewayed ditch which enclosed an area 36m in length by just over 16m

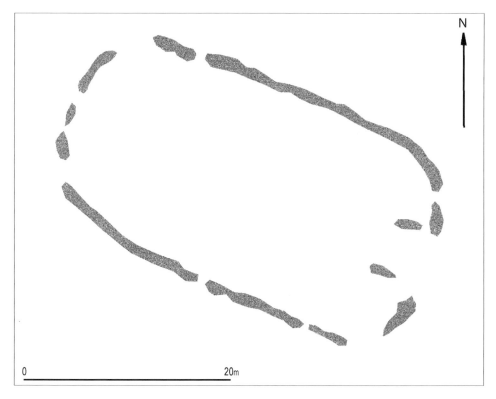

20 The long mortuary enclosure on the slopes of Normanton Down located just 100m south of a long barrow. The discontinuous ditches had an internal bank and there were traces of a wooden structure at the east end. Animal bones and antler picks were recovered from the ditch and a single sherd of Mortlake Ware from a high level. No human remains were recovered and the association of the enclosure with mortuary activities rests upon its similarity to that found beneath the Wor Barrow mound. Antler from the bedding trench produced a radiocarbon date of 3510-2920 (BM-505). *Redrawn from Vatcher 1961*

wide. The upcast from the ditch had been placed internally to create a bank that was still partially visible when originally discovered by Atkinson, though subsequently levelled by cultivation. Internally, the only feature was a pair of short, parallel, bedding trenches set at the eastern end. Each carried three posts and there was some evidence that horizontal timbers had joined them together. Eleven antler picks were the only finds apart from a single sherd of Mortlake Ware, a type of elaborately decorated middle Neolithic pottery, which was found in a secondary position within the ditch fill. The posts were considered to have represented an entrance passage similar to that at Wor Barrow (*21*). It was considered that the enclosure may have been constructed of turf, the evidence of the turf revetting at Holdenhurst and the turf enclosure within Thickthorn Down long barrow being brought to bear as parallels.

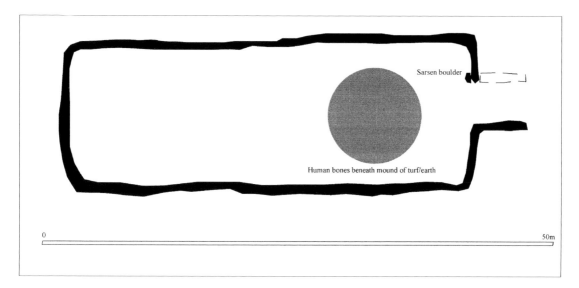

21 A long mortuary enclosure was revealed beneath the mound at Wor Barrow when excavated by Lt General Pitt Rivers in 1893. Towards the east end a low mound of turf covered human remains. *Redrawn from Pitt Rivers 1898*

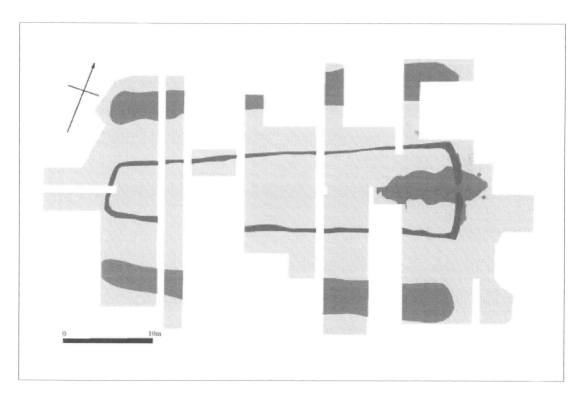

22 Fussell's Lodge excavation plan showing the long mortuary enclosure with cairn overlying human remains situated at the east end. *Redrawn from Ashbee 1966*

The excavation at Fussell's Lodge provided an integral link between long mortuary enclosures and long barrows, although the nature of the association remains uncertain. Whether some long mortuary enclosures originally had an overlying mound that was levelled by cultivation, or a mound was never intended, or whether only certain types of long enclosure, or enclosures in certain areas received mounds is far from clear. What is certain is that the construction of a mound was the final act in the process. It sealed the contents and hid them from view. It provided a break with the past, yet the monumental nature of the construction ensured that the process would be remembered by all involved and its signature would be recognised by those passing through. Analysis of the final form of the monument, the mound itself, therefore, is a convenient place to continue the enquiry.

3

THE SHAPE AND FORM OF
LONG BARROWS

Difference in long barrow form has been recognised since the time of William Cunnington. A glance at the outline plans illustrated in *Figure 8* emphasises that the shapes grade one into another and any categorisation may be an artificial imposition. However, there are certainly enormous differences and a number of prominent distinguishing features. Three basic types of mound can be observed in plan view: trapezoidal, rectangular, and ovoid. There might be a little regional variation, most of those on Salisbury Plain, for example, are wedge-shaped, both mound and ditches being just slightly trapezoidal in outline with one end, usually the easternmost, being the widest. Many are also slightly bulbous around the middle, resulting in less rigidity of geometric form. But this may simply be a result of the detailed study that they have received. Only when Ian Kinnes (1992) investigated regional difference specifically in the ovoid category, where there was a lack of examples in the north, an area that might have more than its share of Neolithic round barrows, was any significant difference noticed. Some long mounds on the Dorset/Wiltshire border with the ditch cutting around one or both ends of the mound have been referred to as the Cranborne Chase type. They are, in fact, more widespread, occurring for example, in Wiltshire, (Sheer Barrow), Oxfordshire (Abingdon) and Sussex (Alfriston), while cropmarks of sites with enclosing ditches are present in Yorkshire (RCHME 1997) and Lincolnshire (Jones, D. 1998). The excavated sites at Skendleby 1 and 2, and West Rudham emphasise that the form may be more frequent in the east than Wessex.

TRAPEZOIDAL BARROWS

The trapezoidal form can be long and slender such as those at Coombe Bissett Farm (*23*), East Down Tilshead, Norton Bavant, Tinhead, all in Wiltshire, or

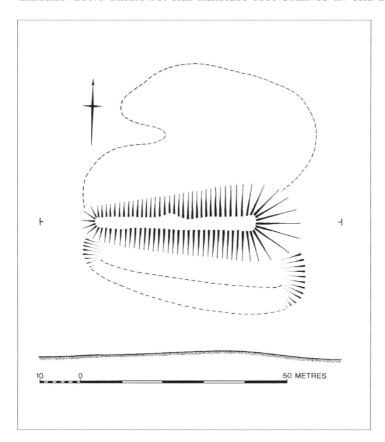

23 Plan of long barrow at Coombe Bissett Farm, Wiltshire, with graceful trapezoidal outline to the mound. © *Crown copyright NMR*

wedge-shaped and a little more stubby such as Boles Barrow, Ell Barrow or Fittleton. The overall taper at Ell Barrow (*24*) and Boles Barrow (*25*) may be the result of two phases of activity as in both cases the mound appears to overlie a platform. Ell Barrow comprises an almost level base platform, broad at the east end, with a long rectangular mound set upon it. The ditches do not taper but one curves slightly to accommodate the platform.

At Fittleton, the wedge form is enhanced by one of the ditches. At Milston, there is a trapezoidal mound on trapezoidal platform (*26*), while at Oxendean, Fittleton, Kill Barrow and White Barrow, ditches were reused and the shape modified during the later Bronze Age, but a bulbous mounding at the easternmost end of the latter site helps to emphasise the trapezoidal plan. Whether this is the result of the presence of a mortuary chamber, or later round barrow addition is unclear, though the expanding ditches neatly encompass the area in each case and suggest that it is an original feature. There are very short examples such as Knook (*27*) and Imber Down, both of which have tapering ditches but a rectangular mound. In these the plan form of the ditches appears to have been as significant as that of the mound.

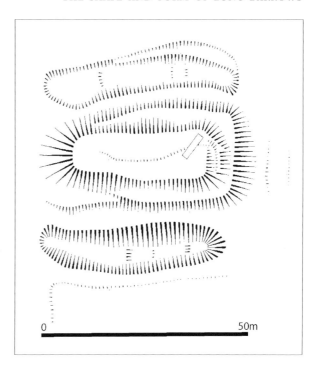

24 Ell Barrow, one of the most prominent barrows on Salisbury Plain Military Training Area is of considerable bulk and, situated within an artillery bombardment zone, has been damaged by 100 years of shelling (not depicted on plan). In recent years the military have kindly removed a large rangefinder from the summit and taken it out of the firing template. When excavated by Thurnam the remains of skeletons were found although the only one mentioned with any detail was a secondary insertion, a large male with a sword wound to the skull. © *Crown copyright NMR*

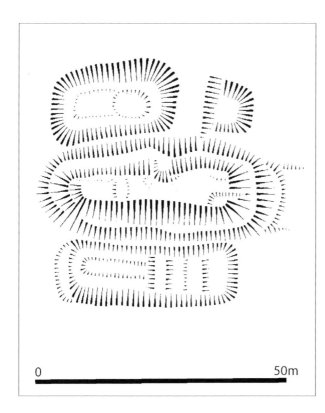

25 Boles Barrow, wedge-shaped with curving side ditches. The mound and ditches have been much disfigured by military activity although it is still possible to make out at least two phases of earthwork. The mound was first excavated by William Cunnington in 1801 who found a pavement of flints on which lay a large number of human bones. Over them was a ridge-shaped cairn of sarsen stones. At the east end were the skulls and horns of at least seven oxen. Thurnam reopened the mound in 1864 and found a secondary interment and Henry and (a later) William Cunnington reinvestigated the mound in 1885 who found further undisturbed primary skeletal material, some of it, they thought, exhibiting signs of violence. © *Crown copyright NMR*

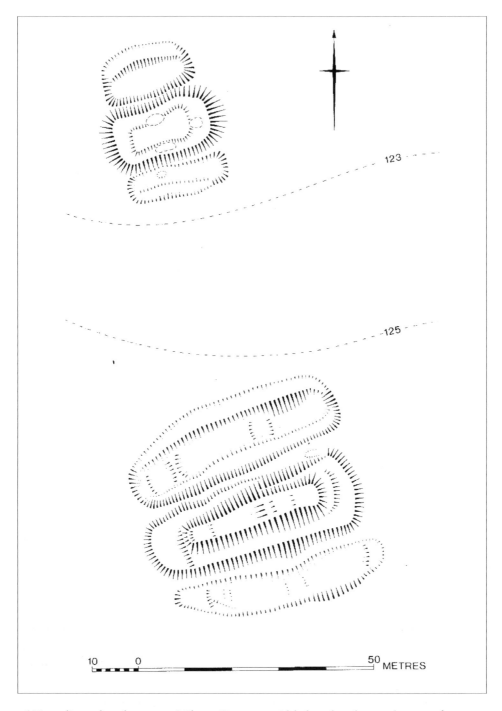

26 Two adjacent long barrows at Milston. One trapezoidal, the other short and rectangular. Phasing can be detected in both long barrows. The trapezoidal example appears to have been constructed on a platform while the shorter example may have had a secondary addition to the summit. © *Crown copyright NMR*

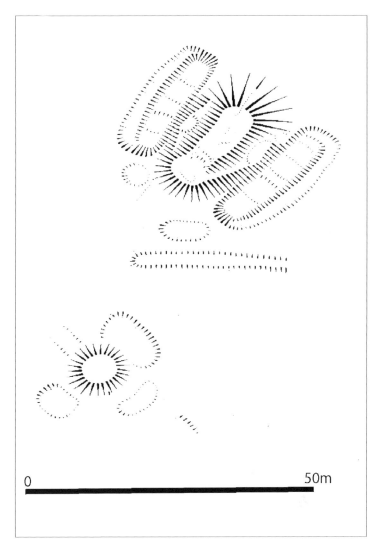

27 Plan of Knook Barrow with a single round mound to the south-west. When excavated by Cunnington charred animal and human bones, of seven or eight individuals, were found on a pavement of flint nodules beneath a flint cairn. On the summit of the cairn lay the skull and horns of an aurochs. © *Crown copyright NMR*

0   50m

RECTANGULAR BARROWS

On Salisbury Plain, only Old Ditch long barrow appears to have been deliberately rectangular and this may be the result of phased construction that masks the original shape (*28*). The ditches are parallel, emphasising that in its final stage at least, a rectangular monument was intended. There has been much subsequent use of the monument that may also have influenced its present form, for example, a number of late Bronze Age linear ditches focus on the mound and these are careful to avoid the Neolithic ditch, but it is also incorporated into a nineteenth-century park boundary and it may even be that the summit of

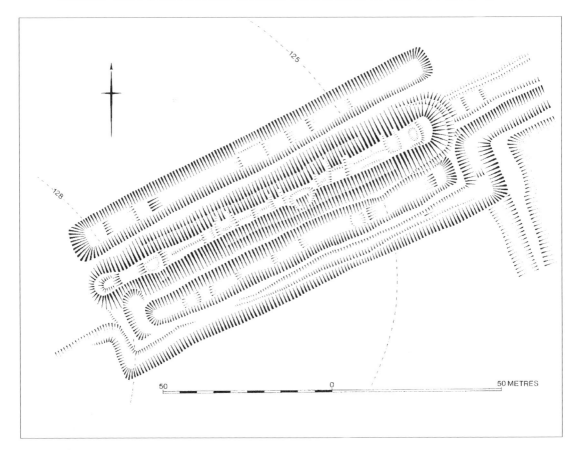

28 One of the finest long barrows on Salisbury Plain, Old Ditch long barrow at Tilshead, Wiltshire is, at 120m in length also one of the longest in the country. However, the eastern end is just slightly more bulbous than the rest of the mound and part of it tapers for about 50m. It is conceivable that the site has been enlarged. Undulations on the summit of the mound may mark the interventions by William Cunnington in 1802 and 1865 by Thurnam. Mound and ditch have provided the focus for a later Bronze Age linear ditch that respects the Neolithic ditch by making clear angled turns. A second linear ditch abuts the first at right angles in the north-east. In historic times the mound was incorporated into a park boundary. © *Crown copyright NMR*

the barrow was levelled to produce a symmetrical surface. A very short example lay alongside a longer barrow on the valley floor at the foot of Beacon Hill at Milston, Wiltshire (26). Other barrows on Salisbury Plain that appear rectangular may have been influenced by cultivation. Heytesbury North Field as the name implies once lay within a cultivated area allowing the ditches to be levelled and the adjacent lynchet created. It now appears as a sub-rectangular mound slightly bulbous around the middle. Similarly at Tilshead Lodge, one of the ditches has been all but levelled and it may be that cultivation has squared off the sides.

OVOID BARROWS

Curving ditches can sometimes give the impression of an ovoid mound. While the ditches at Boles Barrow curve and the platform on which the barrow lies has bulbous sides, the mound as a whole is wedge-shaped. At Round Clump, Whitsbury, a rectangular mound has a curved U-shaped ditch which gives the impression of an oval monument (29). A number of barrows, by no means all, on Cranborne Chase have a ditch that curves around one or both ends and curving ditches define the oval form at Alfriston and Thickthorn Down.

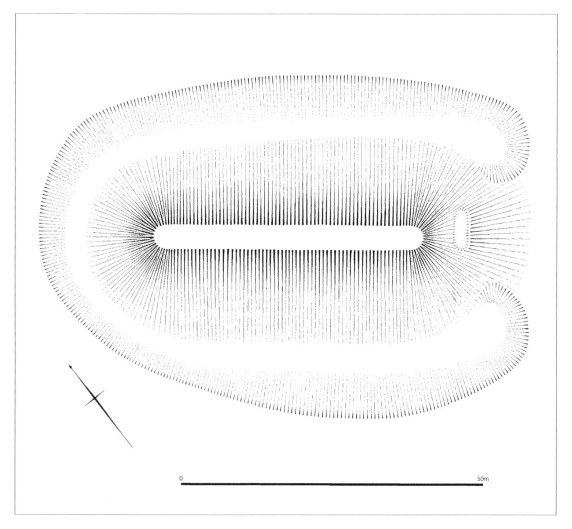

0   50m

29 Although the mound at Round Clump long barrow, Whitsbury, is rectangular, the curving ditches give it an ovoid appearance. © *Crown copyright NMR*

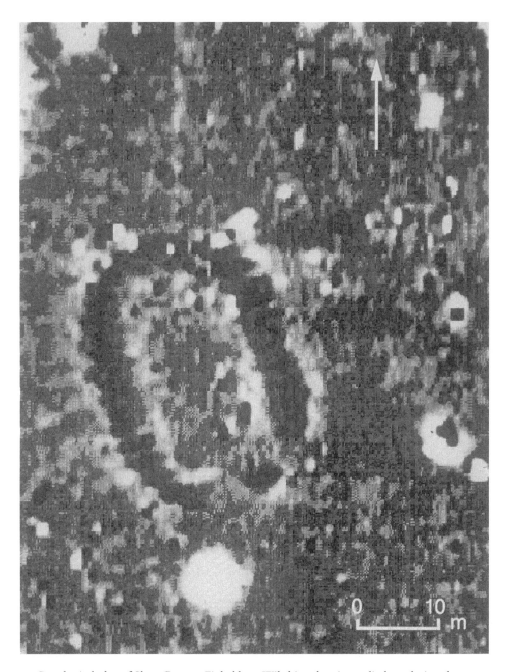

30 Geophysical plot of Sheer Barrow, Figheldean, Wiltshire, showing a ditch enclosing the mound but with a causewayed element in the south. Inside is a sub-rectangular enclosure similar in form to that encountered at Abingdon. © *Crown copyright NMR*

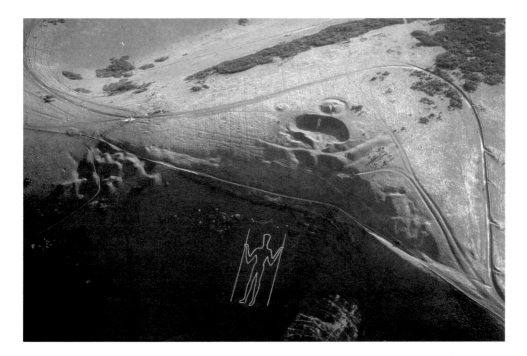

1 Air photograph of Windover Hill in Sussex (NMR 15211/20) showing a long mound adjacent to the large quarry on the summit of the scarp set in the angle of the tramways. It has been suggested that this is a Neolithic long barrow, but the proximity of the quarry spoil encourages caution. © *Crown copyright NMR*

2 The full extent of the long barrow at East Heslerton in Yorkshire can be seen in this air photograph (NMR 17660/20). The broader eastern end to one side of the field boundary was quarried for lime and was excavated by Faith and Lance Vatcher in 1962 revealing a concave façade and part of a mortuary enclosure. © *English Heritage NMR*

3 Cropmarks at Charleston Farm in Yorkshire TA 1370/37 (NMR 17131-23). At 185m this is the longest long barrow in the country, though like other excessively long examples it may result from adding to an earlier monument. Note the flaring ditches (right) and compare with the plan of Old Ditch (28). © *Crown copyright NMR*

4 Air photograph of Long Bredy bank barrow (NMR 18969-05). The break in the mound some 60m from the end may be original and the monument enlarged from a long barrow. Note how the ditch subtly changes course at the same point. © *English Heritage NMR*

5 Air photograph of Chettle long barrow, Dorset (NMR 23822/013). Dug into early in the eighteenth century for the Countess of Temple with 'a great quantity of human bones' found. © *English Heritage NMR*

6 Old Ditch long barrow, at 120m the longest in Wessex. The white wooden posts protect the monument from military vehicles (wood retains heat and is visible using night vision glasses). The trees follow the course of a later Bronze Age linear ditch, itself reused as a park boundary

7 The figures provide scale against the massive bulk of White Barrow, Tilshead

8 Tow barrow lies on the upper slopes of the hill on the far side of Wexcombe valley in Wiltshire. The round barrow on the valley floor marks the site of a spring

9 Tidcombe long barrow, in Wiltshire (NMR 24276/034). Excavation by people from the local village in 1750 probably resulted in the trench at the east end and down the centre of the barrow. They are said to have found a primary burial. Lukis did some excavation at the site of which nothing was reported apart from finding the horn core of an ox. Four sarsens are partly visible at the east end and from this it has been presumed that there was a stone chamber. © *English Heritage NMR*

10 Giants Hills 1 long barrow. Just one of four long barrows or mortuary enclosures set closely together along the side of the valley at Skendleby in Lincolnshire

Left: 11 Winterbourne Stoke Crossroads barrow cemetery with at least eight round mounds adopting the orientation of the long mound (NMR 1041/62). The alignment however, is not precise and more attention appears to have been paid to the landform than the sightline.
© *Crown copyright NMR*

Below: 12 Air photograph of Thickthorn Down (NMR 23822/008). The mound excavated by Drew and Piggott is towards the bottom of the picture. A second long barrow lies just 200m away. The long mound at upper right is the terminal of the Dorset cursus. © *English Heritage NMR*

Above: 13 Pimperne long barrow, Dorset. A massive mound 100m in length situated along a shallow ridge but there is no record of any excavation

Below: 14 Set on the slopes of a basin, the long barrow at Martin's Clump in Hampshire brackets the western limit of the flint mines. Close to the lip of the ditch is a small round barrow similar to those at Wor Barrow

Above: 16 East Kennet long barrow photographed from the air (NMR SU 1166-20). At over 6m in height this is an enormous mound, but like others there are hints in the waisting along its sides that it may have been a two phase monument. © *Crown copyright NMR*

Right: 17 Reconstruction painting of Nutbane long barrow by Mike Codd. The painting illustrates the events as contemporaneous and demonstrates the number of people that must have been involved in construction. Modern interpretation might have posts as free standing and less neat, perhaps carved or painted, or given the influence of Sea-Henge, upturned with roots or branches visible. *Courtesy of the Hampshire Museums and Archives Service*

Opposite: 15 West Kennet stone-chambered long barrow photographed from the air (NMR 15075/15). The cut through the mound at about 30m from the east end may be where two mounds were conjoined as the axial line of the monuments changes slightly at that point. © *Crown copyright NMR*

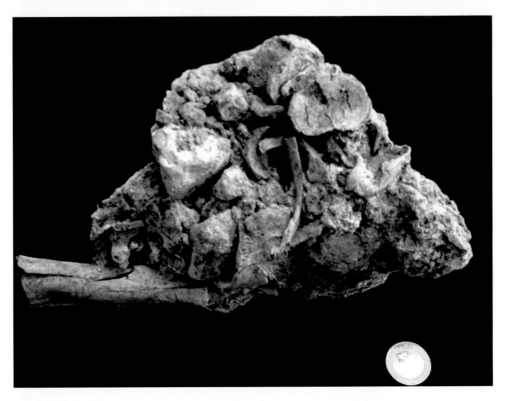

18 A sample of the 'ossiferous breccia' excavated by John Thurnam at Kill Barrow. A fused mass of chalk, splinters of flint, and fractured bone. *Courtesy of the Salisbury and South Wiltshire Museum*

19 Air photograph of cropmarks near Barrow Clump, Ablington, Wiltshire (NMR 15407/08) showing several ring ditches as well as the side ditches and two causewayed segments of a long barrow.
© *Crown copyright NMR*

20 Crop marks on White Hill at Lockeridge overlooking the sarsens in the valley below (NMR 15371/23). The flaring ditches, each about 30m in length, bracket other features, in particular, two large pits or post holes situated adjacent to each other. © *Crown copyright NMR*

21 Longstones long barrow set on the slope just above the valley floor of the Beckhampton stream at Avebury. It is disfigured by chalk digging carried out before the 1720s when Stukeley first observed the mound. Dean Merewether appears to have dug into it in the mid-nineteenth century but there is little record of his discoveries other than of a secondary deposit of a Bronze Age urn and a piece of bronze, probably a spearhead or dagger

22 Spellow Hills long barrow, Lincolnshire. Air photography now indicates that it was just one of four similar Neolithic monuments in the immediate area

23 Adam's Grave, Wiltshire is situated on the scarp edge overlooking the Vale of Pewsey, but it is also prominent from the dip slope to the north where a valley leads towards the sarsens adjacent to White Hill long barrow depicted in *colour plate 20*

24 Vern Ditch long barrow, Hampshire, one of four that line the valley adjacent to the eastern end of the Dorset cursus

25 Deadman's Graves 1 overlooking a narrow valley at Claxby St Andrew, Lincolnshire, is one of two extant barrows located adjacent to each other. A third levelled monument has recently been discovered from the air (by Jones, D. 1998)

26 Pentridge 20 on Bokerley Down, oriented south to north down the slope and dwarfed by the high ground beyond, this is one of four long barrows that line the valley adjacent to the east end of the Dorset cursus

27 Winterbourne Stoke Crossroads long barrow with the road lights at the A303 roundabout just beyond

28 Neolithic carinated lugged bowl showing vertical decoration from the burial area at Fussell's Lodge long barrow. *Courtesy of the Salisbury and South Wiltshire Museum*

29 Therfield Heath long barrow photographed from the air (NMR 23354/34). Nunn's trench along the summit excavated in 1855 can clearly be seen. The later Bronze Age ditch encountered during Phillips (1935) excavation is visible as a dark line at the broader end of the barrow and a small ring ditch can be seen immediately south of the barrow. Nearby are several Bronze Age mounds and elements of a 'Celtic' field system but traces of early activity around the long barrow has been obscured by later cultivation and the construction of golf course earthworks. © *Crown copyright NMR*

30 Kill Barrow from the air (NMR 18135/10). The Later Bronze Age linear ditch utilises Kill Barrow as a marker but respects it and skirts around it. It makes a number of tortuous turns probably to avoid settlement or some other site of importance before continuing across the down cutting through Middle Bronze Age co-axial fields as it does so. The fields were later reused and medieval ridge and furrow is visible across the area. © *Crown copyright NMR*

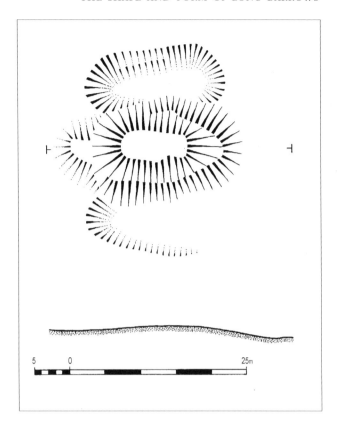

31 Plan of Kitt's Grave, Broad Chalke, Wiltshire. © *Crown copyright NMR*

The rounded corners of the ditch provide an oval shape to the monument at, for example, Sheer Barrow, where a slight, currently oval, mound remains extant, although a survey by Bradford Geophysical Surveys indicated that it contained a sub-rectangular mortuary enclosure (*30*). Moody's Down, Hampshire, has one curved and one straight ditch flanking an asymmetrical mound.

Short barrows are by no means necessarily oval. One of the shortest at just over 19m is Wilsford 13 on Normanton Down, which may have been rectangular and is dwarfed by the adjacent round barrows. Another at Milston, Wiltshire, little more than 25m in length, has a rectangular mound and parallel ditches. The short barrows at Kingston Deverill, Wiltshire and Suddern, Hampshire, have expanding ditches, and one might therefore expect to see a trapezoidal mound and it is possible that the oval mound at the latter site is a result of cultivation. Expanding ditches at Kitt's Grave, Wiltshire (*31*) flank an amorphous mound evidently of two phases. A number of mounds are short and stubby, for example, Knook Down long barrow is just 25m in length, while Knook Barrow itself reaches only 30m; the latter comprising a combination of architectural features, tapering ditches, the mound sub-rectangular but with a bulbous north-eastern end.

32 Wor Barrow showing the form of the mound set on the then open countryside of Cranborne Chase with excavation of the ditch underway. *Photograph: Pitt Rivers 1898*

Following the excavation of a mound at North Marden in Sussex, Peter Drewett (1975) suggested that oval mounds of less than 40m in length may form a discrete 'late' type in Sussex, but both size and form extend beyond Sussex. The ditch form of Wor Barrow (*32*) is not dissimilar from that at Marden while Whitsbury, in Hampshire might also fall into the category, as might Thickthorn Down and Wayland's Smithy 1.

SIZE

The length of mound varies quite dramatically, from the massive Old Ditch, at Tilshead, in Wiltshire, which reaches 120m to Wilsford 13, on Normanton Down, which at 19m is among the smallest. Most lie within the 25-75m range, with 50m being around the norm. Unfortunately such measurements can only be a guide, for surface length is easily affected by cultivation. The Tinhead long barrow, Wiltshire, for example, once measured some 77m in length, but now reaches just 62m, while the Middleton Down example has been reduced from 55m to just 30m. Some barrows are unusually long. East and West Kennet, as well as East Heslerton in Yorkshire, exceed 100m and, like Old Ditch, approach the length of bank barrows. However, as noted above, in all cases there are slight hints in the plan that they may have been enlarged from more average-sized mounds.

The width of the mound is less prone to plough truncation, as the flanking ditch will often provide some protection. The maximum width is 30m at Round Clump in Hampshire, 28m at White Barrow. These are extreme figures and it usually lies between 12m and 23m, most often occurring at the easternmost end.

The height varies quite dramatically between 1-3.5m and is also often greater at the easternmost end. East Kennet reaches an enormous 6.6m. Many, however,

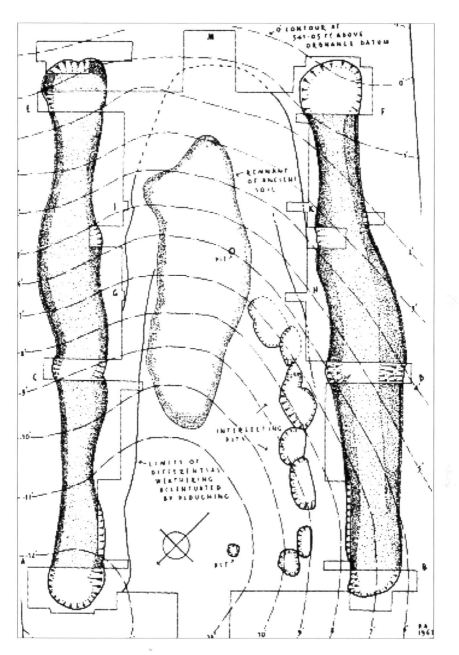

33 Excavation plan of Horslip long barrow, set on the lower southern slopes of Windmill Hill, Avebury, parallel to the Yatesbury stream just 200m away. *Courtesy of Paul Ashbee*

34 Excavation trenches at Horslip long barrow, Windmill Hill, Avebury. *Courtesy of Paul Ashbee*

especially when reduced by cultivation, are of lesser proportions, although it is by no means clear from the surface evidence whether the full height of the mound itself is necessarily being observed, or the partly shielded and unweathered natural chalk surface. Where unprotected by overburden, the chalk surface has dissolved considerably since the Neolithic, being truncated by 0.5m or more. When excavated the 0.6m high mound at Horslip, on the slopes of Windmill Hill, near Avebury, Wiltshire, there was demonstrated to be a platform of natural chalk that had been protected from weathering by the mound remnant (*33* and *34*). Analysis of the height of mounds on Salisbury Plain indicates that they fall into two general categories, those of about 1m or waist height and those above 2.5-3m (McOmish *et al.* 2002), that is, those that you look up to. It's not simply that there is a difference in shape or length, but in overall bulk. Some mounds are absolutely enormous when compared to others of very similar form. It is as though certain monuments have been deliberately made *monumental*. It is the combination of large measurements, King Barrow at Warminster (*14*), for example, is 62m in length, 17m wide and 4.5m in height, that gives certain mounds this bulk.

Many mounds of more slender build would, in cultivated areas, be easily eradicated. Fortunately, those in the military training area of Wiltshire such as Heytesbury North Field or Durrington Down have been protected from the destruction of the twentieth century, although so many have been affected by ancient or medieval cultivation. Mounds close to historic settlements and within their areas of cultivation tend to fare worst, for example Sheer Barrow at Figheldean, Wiltshire, or the barrow on Imber Down. Those that survive are often at a distance from historic settlement foci, to where it was difficult or not worthwhile sending plough teams. Boles Barrow or Kill Barrow for example, or as at Wor Barrow, where the mound has been incorporated into a parish boundary. This is true of many monuments not just barrows, Romano-British monuments on Salisbury Plain survive because of their distance from village centres, while Grimes Graves in Norfolk, situated at the junction of three parish boundaries, survives for the same reason.

PROFILE

Further categorisation might take into account the profile. Many, particularly those of trapezoidal plan, are tapered in profile with one end, frequently the easternmost, being higher than the other. Sometimes this is quite dramatic, but on other occasions more subtle. Some, particularly rectangular examples, have a level profile while others, such as White Barrow are 'pyriform' or pear-shaped, parabolic, or as Cunnington wrote, 'like an egg cut in two lengthways'. Assuming they were to be viewed from the valley below it is the side view or profile that appears to have been important. Some, particularly those situated on the ridges between the streams close to the spring line on Cranborne Chase almost mimic the topography, while others can appear as prone animals. Bearing in mind that the mound covers earlier architectural features, it seems likely that the external form, in part at least, is likely to mirror what is buried within.

ORIENTATION

In a letter to H.P. Wyndham in August 1801, Cunnington recorded that Boles Barrow was erected to meet the four cardinal points and the orientation of mounds has figured prominently in description and analysis ever since. Both Ashbee and Kinnes have catalogued the variation, which is generally from north-east to south-east, although there are a number oriented from north to south. As noted above, in almost all cases the larger end lies towards the east and undoubtedly there is a cosmological implication, probably associated with solar or lunar observations. The Winterbourne Stoke Crossroads long barrow (*colour plate 11*) is oriented on midsummer sunrise as is Beckhampton Road; however, both are also oriented with the lie of the land and in the case of the latter the horizon is obscured by Folly Hill. It is invariably the case that barrows respect the contours. Rarely does one cut across, although there are occasional examples such as Jullieberrie's Grave in Kent and Woodford long barrow in Wiltshire that do so, both are oriented to the north and there are long cairns at Dyffryn Ardudwy and Tan-y-muriau on the slopes of Mynydd Rhiw in north Wales, which are also oriented downhill. However, often the east to west alignment simply reflects the local topography. West Kennet, for example, mirrors the orientation of the Kennet Valley, while nearby mounds at South Street and Beckhampton Road are angled east to west and north-eastwards respectively as the contours are so aligned. On Cranborne Chase, where the rivers Allen and Tarrant cut southwards, mounds, for example, Thickthorn Down (*colour plate 12*), Pimperne (*colour plate 13*), Gussage Hill and Wor Barrow are similarly oriented along the interfluves. An exception here is the Chettle long barrow which takes the orientation of the spur on which it is situated.

DITCHES

In general the ditches mimic or help define the plan shape of the mound, serving to accentuate its form. Where the body of the mound is straight, the flanking ditches are also often straight and where ovoid the ditches tend to be curved. Given the extent to which the ditches were re-cut at causewayed enclosures, such procedures might be expected at long barrows too. Slight ledges visible within some ditches, at for example, Boles Barrow, Norton Bavant, Knook, Alton Down or East Down at Tilshead, might be an indication of this, although caution must always be applied, as in some cases this might simply be the result of weathering. Ditches are invariably between 15-20m in width at the surface. White Barrow and Old Ditch both have ditches that are 20m wide and, like the mounds, some are of markedly greater proportions than others. In contrast, the ditches at Danebury East are less than 10m wide and at Martin's Clump in Hampshire, just 5m (*colour plate 14*).

Long barrows provide the earliest evidence of ditch digging and given the architecture of causewayed enclosures, current from about 3600 cal. BC, it might be a little surprising that so few ditches are composed of pits or are significantly causewayed. One of the ditches at Badshot Lea, Farnham, has a causeway towards the west end. The ditch at Wor Barrow is broken by causeways, that in the south-east being wider than the others, perhaps signalling the presence of an entrance into the interior. Sheer Barrow has two causeways at the south-eastern narrow end and Thickthorn Down and Skendleby 1 a single causeway in the north-west corner. Where causeways occur, the usual location is towards either of the ends, where they might mark a decision to curtail the length of the mound as short barrows appear to have a greater incidence of causewayed ditches. Alfriston has a single causeway at the east end; the southernmost ditch at Kingston Deverill has a single causeway, while North Marden has six, the smaller segments at the narrow ends of the mound. The northern ditch at Boles Barrow is discontinuous but this is a result of more recent activity. Recent excavations at Amesbury 42, situated alongside the eastern terminal of the Stonehenge cursus, demonstrated that the ditch was of two phases. The earlier was a causewayed round-bottomed ditch of about 1.4m in width and 1.3m deep. It probably silted up naturally and may have had an internal bank and was partially cut into by a flat-bottomed ditch of far greater proportions, about 4m in width and some 2.2m deep. Two phases of ditch digging were recorded at East Heslerton (Vatcher 1965), but it is not clear whether either was interrupted. The southern ditch of the smaller of the two long barrows on Hambledon Hill was also re-cut (Healy 2004) and such re-cutting may have been more widespread than currently reported.

In each case, the ditch appears to be a fully intended design feature; an integral part of the final appearance. On Salisbury Plain, a few barrows, Fittleton for example, have slightly asymmetrical ditches but this may sometimes be the result

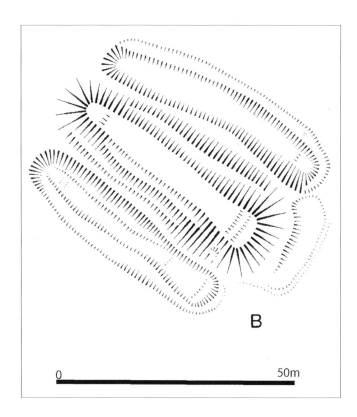

35 Plan of East Down long Barrow, Tilshead in Wiltshire, with some phasing in the body of the slender trapezoidal mound and asymmetrical appearance due to the curving northern ditch. © Copyright NMR

0   50m

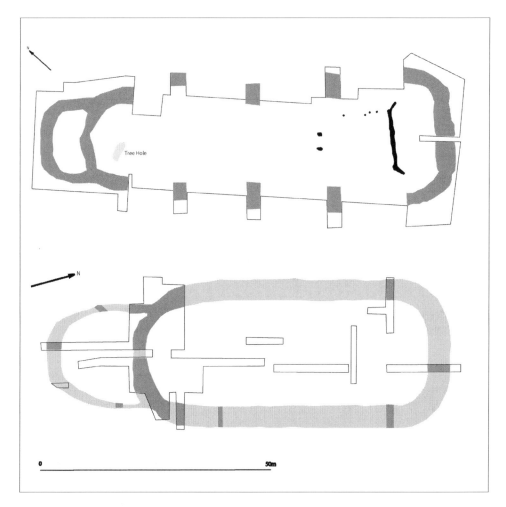

36 Excavation plans of Giants Hills 2, Skendleby, Lincolnshire (above: *redrawn from Evans and Simpson 1991*) and West Rudham, Norfolk (below: *redrawn from Hogg 1941*). Both are encompassed by a continuous ditch and in each case the mound appears to have been extended at the distal end. Note how the façade trench depicted on the Skendleby plan lies on a different orientation to both the ditch and the pair of pits that flanked the burials

of later activity. Only at Ell Barrow and East Down (*35*) does asymmetry appear to have been part of the original build and even then perhaps not intended.

At both Skendleby long barrows the ditch encompassed the mound. At Giant's Hills 2, it appears to have been extended to lengthen the area enclosed, while at Giant's Hills 1 just a narrow causeway was left at the north-east corner of the mound (*36* and *37*). When excavated, the latter ditch was found to have been 3.5m deep and 3.5m wide, becoming both shallower and narrower towards each end. A considerable part of it was excavated but beyond

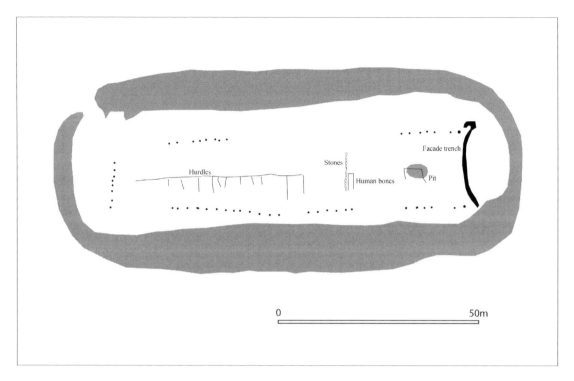

37 Excavation plan of Giants Hills 1, Skendleby, Lincolnshire with the concave façade trench at the east end. A platform with human bones on it lay a little east of the centre bracketed on one side by a low 'wall' of stones. East of this was a 'ritual' pit over which part of the hurdle arrangement appears to have been placed. The hurdle bays were only recorded on one side of the mound at the west end, although they might have extended for the full length and perhaps on both sides. The stake holes around the perimeter are thought to have revetted the mound but may also have secured the outer edge of the hurdle bays. *Redrawn from Philips 1936*

a few small fragments of deer antler, sherds of Neolithic pottery and some unretouched flint flakes, little was found in terms of cultural deposits. Phillips inferred that as the chalk and loam covering the mound, presumed to have derived from the ditch, was placed in an irregular manner rather than being placed on the ground in reverse order, the ditches had been dug in a localised and erratic fashion.

BERMS

Berms, now obscured by weathering of the ditch edge and soil creep from the mound, can be quite narrow and negligible, even where the original form may have been crisp and well defined. Most are 3m in width, but can reach what seems to be an excessive width, 10m at Nutbane and Imber Down. The latter monument, however, lay close to the village of Imber in a formerly cultivated area and it may be that the mound itself was once wider. Nevertheless the distances are too large in some instances to indicate that the purpose was to ensure that mound material did not easily fall into the ditch and it may be that the space between the ditches played an unknown but important factor in ceremonies.

VISIBLE CHRONOLOGY

A number of barrows contain barely perceptible breaks of slope or ledges that might indicate phases of activity or use. They need not be prehistoric, but in many cases are likely to be. In some cases the mound appears to have been constructed over a platform often no more than 0.25m in height. It may be that this relates to the dissolution of the surrounding chalk, as occurred around Horslip and is an entirely natural phenomenon, however, if so one might expect the chalk of the platform to have dissolved in a similar way. It may have resulted from historical weathering of the mound material itself; alternatively it may be the result of phased construction of the barrow and may represent visible parts of an underlying mortuary enclosure, or an early phase of barrow construction only later *monumentalised* by covering with a massive mound. The mound at Ell Barrow lies on such a platform (*24*), the curve on the north of which is reflected by the ditch on that side. Boles Barrow and Knook Barrow both appear to be constructed on platforms, as does Norton Bavant where there also appears to be additional phasing at the smaller end. Earthwork scarping at Fittleton suggests that there may be an underlying feature and there is also some evidence of heightening at the narrow end and similar phasing may occur at the smaller end of White Barrow. The longer of the two barrows at Milston occupies a well-defined trapezoidal platform (*26*). The mound proper lies short of both platform and the ditches at either end. While it could be that there was an attempt to level the extremities of the mound at some time in the past, it appears to be an original feature.

Analysis of the earthworks provides a slight indication that some of the larger mounds may be the result of conjoining barrows. Enlargement by building one mound on top of another is known from Wayland's Smithy, where excavations by Richard Atkinson demonstrated that a large trapezoidal mound was built over a smaller ovoid one (Atkinson 1965). At the well-known stone-chambered barrow at West Kennet (*colour plate 15*), the mound is twice the usual length of a long barrow, but broadening occurs at about 55m from the west end. Coupled with a subtle change in direction of the ditch at this point, it may in fact be two contiguous barrows (Brown *et al.* 2005). The same may be true of East Kennet (*colour plate 16*), where a waisting half way along the 101m long mound occurs. The trapezoidal feature at the eastern end of the massive Old Ditch has already been mentioned, while Richard Bradley (1983) has suggested that the Long Bredy, Maiden Castle and Pentridge bank barrows may in fact be extended long barrows.

Only rarely are long barrows associated directly with round barrows. Additions to the summit of mounds in later periods might be expected. The possibility that the raised area at the east end of White Barrow is a Bronze Age round barrow has already been entertained. Excavation at some, for example, Beckhampton Road and Kilham, has demonstrated the presence of others.

Confusion on this count has led to some monuments being discredited as long barrows. The mound south of Woodhenge originally thought to be a long barrow is now thought to comprise three confluent round barrows set on a ridge of chalk (RCHME 1979b). A number of former long barrows were excluded from the category in Hampshire, perhaps most interesting is that at Down Grange, Basingstoke, where a curious arrangement of small confluent round mounds set over an elongated oval ditch (RCHME 1979a); perhaps a long mortuary enclosure. At Martin's Clump a small round mound immediately adjacent to the lip of the ditch may be Bronze Age, but in view of the proximity of similar sized mounds at Wor Barrow there is a possibility that it is Neolithic. There may be Romano-British or Saxon additions as well. This appeared to be the case at Westow, in Yorkshire, where broadening of the mound was attributed to later activity (Greenwell 1877, 490-7). A slight heightening of one side of the summit at Ell Barrow may be a result of Saxon activity given the secondary material that has come from the mound, although damage by the military may equally be responsible.

In some instances subtle undulations on the surface of the mound might indicate internal features, but certainty can only be achieved by excavating into the interior. There is evidence of more recent, probably antiquarian digging in a number of mounds, such as Norton Bavant and Alton Down, Longwood at Owslebury, and Long Burgh, Sussex. Localised quarrying by farmers or others is widespread and has cut into the mounds at Tinhead and Bratton. There are transverse cuts at West Kennet and Longwood, where material has been removed, and there possibly would have been at King Barrow if the farmer had continued with plans uninfluenced by Cunnington. The surface of the mound has been cut into for chalk at Preston Candover and Giant's Grave, Breamore and quarrying of the underlying chalk as well has resulted in disfigurement at Badshot Lea, Surrey, Woodcutt, Hampshire, and East Heslerton, Yorkshire.

It is difficult to imagine how the original appearance of the mound, in its unweathered state might have been perceived. Construction of the mound was the final part in the process. In some cases, at for example, Fussell's Lodge, filling in the long mortuary enclosure formed the first part of the process. At Haddenham, the wooden structures were covered by clay, presumably dug from the ditch and this was covered by a considerable deposit of turf before finally being capped by a deposit of gravel (Hodder and Shand 1988, 352). The final capping is mirrored at Raunds which was also covered with gravel and is a process difficult to account for. It may have been to do with colour. Those barrows situated on the chalk, once capped will have appeared brilliant white for a considerable period of time after construction and it may be that the gravel was designed to emulate that.

4

THE STRUCTURE OF
LONG BARROWS

The results of excavations accumulated over 200 years have demonstrated that the earthen long barrow masks a sequence of activity on each site and indeed building of the mound often appears to be the final act, sealing and disguising what went before. Its construction signals an alteration in the way that the location was used and understood; allowing the introduction of changed uses and the knowledge of formerly visible structures, remains and events could only be confined to memory. The excavations provide some details of these structures although interpreting their purpose is rather more difficult.

How each area was used prior to construction is largely unknown. There are indications of much earlier activity at a number of sites; sometimes just a few pieces of flintwork, in other cases the presence of pits and hearths. Two patinated microliths were recovered at South Street, Wiltshire, one a lanceolate point, came from the pre-barrow soil (Ashbee *et al.*1979). Several patinated Mesolithic flints were also found in the ditch of the Horslip long barrow on the slopes of Windmill Hill, Avebury, nearby (Ashbee *et al.*1979, 218). On other occasions more substantial amounts of material have been recorded. Beneath the long barrow at Kilham in Yorkshire lay an extensive late Mesolithic flint scatter that focused around a series of hearths and pits. The nature of these is unclear. There is no apparent order to them and there were no indications of postholes. One, designated Pit B, contained some small fragments of animal (large ox) and possibly human bone, with charred hazelnut shells in the overlying soil. A second also contained small fragments of animal bone (Manby 1976, 117). Centuries later such partially silted or backfilled pits would have been visible as earthworks and, together with the scatter of patinated artefacts, recognised as the remnants of human behaviour. Whether they acted as a focus for subsequent activity is unclear, but in turn a series of Neolithic pits were added to the site.

Beneath the mound at Thickthorn Down, and sealed by the old ground surface was an alignment of three pits set on a north-easterly axis. The later mound utilised one of them for its central axis suggesting that it was marked on the surface in some way. The pits were of irregular form, the smallest just *c.*1.5m across and the largest 3m. The depth is not recorded, but Drew and Piggott, the excavators, indicated that they were filled with chalk rubble and odd burnt flints and pieces of charcoal. They considered that as a turf line had developed over them they must have been considerably earlier than the barrow. From one came a flint core, while a microlith was found on the old land surface nearby. One of the pits contained six fragments of pine charcoal and there were also traces of pear, apple, possibly plum or cherry (Drew and Piggott 1936). Whether they once held posts is unclear, for given the pine charcoal it might be tempting to compare them with the three postholes found at Stonehenge and dated to the Mesolithic period (Cleal *et al.* 1995).

At the western end of Skendleby 1, a number of small and shallow ditches were encountered that appear to have silted up naturally (Phillips 1936, 74). One lay at right angles to the main ditch. Another is thought to have existed along the outer side of the northern ditch with a further example on the inner side for part of its course. All were fully silted before the barrow was constructed and the ditches dug. It is possible that these features were visible as earthworks and influenced the course of later structural details but no cultural material was recovered and although fragments of charcoal were recovered the excavation took place before the advent of radiocarbon dating.

PREPARATION OF GROUND

Remarkably, beneath the mound at South Street, Avebury, excavations by John Evans revealed a series of criss-cross grooves interpreted as ard- or plough-marks situated at right angles to each other (*38*). The grooves were some 0.3m apart and scored deeply into the chalk subsoil and were thought to represent more than one episode of cultivation. Clearance of stones and boulders had taken place and the ard may have broken up the soil prior to cultivation, while the soil profile indicated subsequent tillage, possibly using hoes or spades. A C14 date from charcoal found on the old ground surface above the marks provided a date of 3100-2550 cal. BC at 95 per cent probability, that is, relatively late in terms of long barrow chronology. The marks were on a north-north-west orientation and at right angles to it, which is at odds with the orientation of the later barrow. Surface earthworks, therefore, did not appear to have influenced barrow position or orientation. However, a line of stake holes of unexplained purpose found

38 Criss-cross ard-marks
found beneath the
mound at South Street.
*Courtesy of the Alexander
Keiller Museum, Avebury*

beneath the barrow may have been associated in some way. It has been suggested that the episode of clearance and ploughing was to ritually prepare the ground for construction of the monument (Rowley Conwy 1987: contra Kristiansen 1990). However, the soil profile shows that the area reverted to grassland immediately before construction and the ploughed area neglected. The barrow was therefore constructed on an abandoned, perhaps ancestral cultivation plot, and possibly situated towards the edge of the ploughed area. If the community were located close to water it would imply settlement alongside the Kennet stream, in which case placing the barrow at the edge of cultivated land served to demarcate limits of the land holding.

South Street was not the only barrow built on an old field, for at Kilham there were two phases of cultivation noted in the pre-barrow soil profile (Manby 1976) while both Dalladies and Pitnacree were also sited on formerly cultivated land (Piggott 1971, 45-6). 'Mechanical disturbance' in the buried soil at Fussell's Lodge was reported (Cornwall in Ashbee 1966, 74) but this cannot be put down to cultivation with any certainty. At a second mound excavated at Skendleby, Giant's Hills 2, it was thought that the barrow was also built close to the edge of cultivated land, where like South Street, there was a short period of grassland prior to construction and Beckhampton Road long barrow also had 'arable nearby' (Ashbee *et al.* 1979, 244). Grassland was noted beneath Willerby Wold long barrow (Manby 1963), Alfriston (Thomas in Drewett *et al.* 1975) and probably at Horslip, while at Amesbury 42, at the eastern end of the Stonehenge cursus, grassland also appears to have been present for some time before the mound was built (Entwistle in Richards 1990, 105-108).

More recently, work by Alasdair Whittle at Easton Down long barrow, Bishops Cannings, Wiltshire, has served to confirm the general trend. While woodland was present on the higher chalk downs, pollen indicated that the mound itself was in open grassland close to the edge of a formerly cultivated area (Whittle *et al.* 1993).

Such influence on the natural environment will have evolved through millennia of interaction. The impact of herds of red deer coupled with grazing by aurochs may have resulted in considerable tracts of countryside being quite open. Indeed, the vegetation cover of parts of the Wessex downland may have been relatively open from an early date and some places may have remained open from the end of the last glaciation (French *et al.* 2003) as grazing animals coupled with aspect and climate conspired to ensure that vegetation was restricted.

There is some indication at Alfriston that turf and topsoil may have been stripped from the ground surface prior to mound construction. (Thomas in Drewett *et al.* 1975, 148-150). If so, it may have been to level the site. Such procedures may have occurred at other sites also, for example, Silbury Hill, where truncation of the chalk appears to have taken place beneath part of the mound.

PITS

Consistently reported as lying beneath internal cairns or mounds, single 'cists' or pits were clearly among the earliest of features. Occasionally there was more than one. Rarely did they contain diagnostic artefacts or indeed any cultural debris at all and where they did it was merely a few fragments of charcoal or burnt bone. The absence of obvious explanation led to them being referred to as 'ritual' pits (Philips 1935). There were other sites such as Corton, where Cunnington encountered two pits at the base of the mound, each over a metre in diameter and approximately 0.7m deep, both neatly cut into the underlying chalk. Like most of those excavated beneath other barrows, neither contained cultural material, but between them lay eight human skeletons. The excavations at Fussell's Lodge and Nutbane long barrows during the 1950s shed further light on this. At each, postholes were interpreted as forming wooden burial chambers which introduced the possibility that early investigators had missed other pits and misinterpreted them. Additional support for this came from the excavation of Skendleby 2, which revealed the presence of two pits with D-shaped post-casts, situated transversely to the axis of the mound and like Corton, with human bone deposited between them.

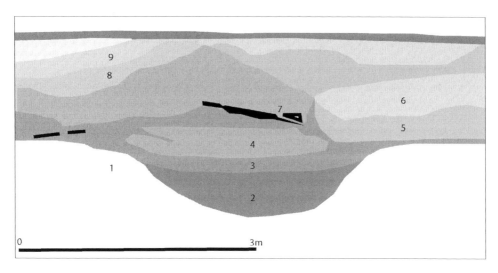

39 Simplified section drawing of the 'ritual' pit beneath Giants Hills 1, Skendleby. *Redrawn from Philips 1936*

However, this contrasted with the evidence from Skendleby 1, situated little more than 200m away and extensively excavated by C.W. Philips in 1934 (1936). There, a single pit, oval in plan and measuring a quite substantial 3.3 x 2.1m, was cut into the original ground surface to a depth of 0.9m towards the easternmost end on the central axis of the later mound. It contained no cultural material, but had been filled almost to the surface with clean, white, chalk rubble (*39*). Since a stake fence cut into this deposit and the arrangement was covered by mound material, it appeared to represent amongst the earliest of activities on the site. Above the filling was a thin layer of midden material containing minute pieces of pottery, bone, flint, charcoal and fragments of carbonised hazelnut and seeds, which was all thought to have been brought from an off-site location. Given the degree to which the central part of the mound was investigated there seems to have been little scope for an undiscovered companion pit of similar dimensions.

Many of the other Wiltshire examples were similar. Cunnington often described how they were carefully and neatly cut into the underlying chalk. At Heytesbury North Field, a pit measuring approximately 1.5m in diameter and 0.7m deep was empty of artefacts but filled with the same material as that of the overlying circular mound. Beneath Knook 2, the pit, situated close to the centre of the barrow, was semi-circular, evidently deliberately backfilled with earth and the shape inviting suggestions that it held a split trunk. At Knook Down, the pit was circular and nearly 0.9m deep, but it also contained two bone fragments and pieces of charcoal, while at Old Ditch, an oval pit, 0.9m long by 0.5m wide by 0.75m deep, was 'cut with such exactness in the solid marl as though it had

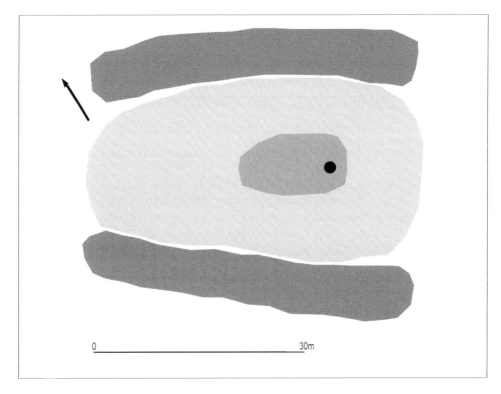

0 _____ 30m

40 Sketch plan of Moody's Down long barrow. The mound was destroyed in 1940 when a rifle range was recorded but Grimes was able to piece together the salient details from observers. A pit situated towards the south-east end was filled and covered by flint nodules. To the west of the pit were the remains of a skeleton and these features were in turn covered by an internal mound of black soil. *Redrawn from Grimes 1960*

been done by a chisel' but contained nothing but earth and charred wood. Only on one occasion, at Sherrington, on the gravels of the flood plain terrace of the River Wylye, did the pit contain significant material, an ox skull and a small piece of antler.

Such pits formed an important component elsewhere. During levelling of the south-east long barrow on Moody's Down, Hampshire for a rifle range in 1940, observers of the destruction noted that a pit was present towards the south-east end filled and covered with a pile of flints (*40*). Unfortunately, little else is known of it (Grimes 1960, 248-9). Beneath Therfield Heath long barrow, at Royston, Hertfordshire, were two pits excavated in 1855 by E. B. Nunn, one of which contained 'ashes' (*41*). They were cut into the underlying chalk and lay just over 5m apart on an east to west alignment, an axis later utilised in the construction of the barrow mound. Commenting on them, Phillips described them as 'ritual pits' (Phillips 1935, 106). They may have provided a focus for burial activity and one

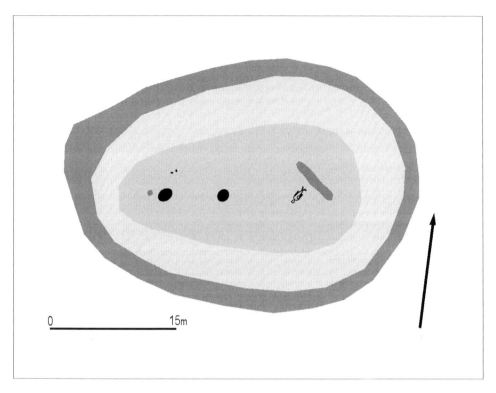

41 Therfield Heath long barrow with features excavated by Nunn (1855) and Phillips (1935)

might have expected human remains to lie between them in a similar manner to Corton and Skendleby 2, but the only human bone reported as being found was considerably west of the pits.

At least one early pit lay beneath the Nutbane long barrow in Hampshire. It was oval, measuring approximately 1 x 0.75m and 0.3m deep and contained only dark soil. A burial had been placed over it. A second pit of similar dimensions lay 2m to the east-north-east, on the same alignment as the later barrow and was thought to have contained a post. The two were interpreted as forming part of a free-standing post arrangement subsequently used as a mortuary structure (Morgan 1959). Excavated in 1957 at the same time as Nutbane, a not dissimilar circumstance occurred at Fussell's Lodge although this produced a rather different ground plan it was readily interpreted as a mortuary structure. Two and possibly three oval pits were found oriented slightly north of east, the same alignment as the later barrow. Like Nutbane, burials covered one of the pits, but the overlying bones had settled into the top of it. Paul Ashbee concluded that a post had been withdrawn resulting in the settlement of the overlying human bones. The third, deeper pit considered to be later in date was cut into the entrance gap in the façade in a similarly problematic position to that at Willerby Wold (Ashbee 1966, 1-80), where at least one, and possibly two 'ritual' pits, were set 2m apart, the second evidently pre-dating, but also forming a component of, the façade. The façade here had been cut into by an overlying crematorium and partly filled by fused chalk (Manby 1963).

The crucial question is whether and to what extent many of these pits represent postholes, and where they do what kind of structure is represented. Like a number of sites, at Heytesbury North Field, the pit was filled with the same material that formed the overlying circular internal mound, and this would appear to link the two events. If the pit had formerly held a post it must have been retrieved.

It is possible that some of the pits were used in other ways. At Arn Hill, Warminster, for example, an irregular sarsen stone standing to more than 1.5m in height with its pointed end in the ground was found in the position where a pit was found on other sites. To the south and south-east of it lay a crude pavement of chalk blocks on which lay the bones of two adults and a child with heads to the east. There are other cases where this occurred. Four standing stones on a north-east alignment underlay a long cairn on Skelmore Head in Cumbria (Powell *et al.* 1963). Aubrey mentions a standing stone at the east end of Leighterton long barrow, near Nailsworth (Fowles 1980, 816), while Thurnam noted cases of monoliths or 'triliths' at the wide end of some' chambered' long barrows. At the false entrance at Ablington, Gloucestershire, a massive stone 1.8m by 1.5m, kept in position by a further, perforated stone, was sealed between two concentric curving lengths of dry stone walls, while at Avening, also in Gloucestershire, a massive standing stone is referred to as the 'Tingle stone'.

PAVEMENTS

Situated immediately adjacent to many such pits is a pavement of stones on which skeletal material was invariably placed. Proximity is explicitly noted by Cunnington on several occasions, but the best recorded example is at Skendleby 1, where a carefully placed rectangular pavement of chalk blocks laid on the original ground surface was described as 'crazy paving'. Almost 3m by just over 1m in width, it was set at right angles to the long axis of the monument; its western edge partially defined by a kerb of flint nodules and small boulders set on edge. One boulder of slightly larger size was difficult to move and having examined a fragment, J.K. St Joseph indicated that it was from the Melrose area, that is to say, it had been purposefully collected and placed. The boulder kerb and area to the west of them were subsequently covered by a pile of midden material 3m wide and almost 1m thick, which contained minute pieces of bone, pottery, flint, charcoal and part of a small bone chisel, all thought to represent imported occupation debris. Four crouched skeletons were present on the pavement along with further bones representing parts of four other bodies. They were closely packed together, overlaying each other and were strictly confined to the area of the pavement.

Regularly laid flint nodules formed the pavement at Boles Barrow, on which lay 'the remains of a great many human bodies'. The description implies that this was no scattering of nodules but something carefully constructed. The pavement of flints discovered at the west end of Old Ditch long barrow was about 0.5m above the old ground surface laying on the 'black earth'. On this too, lay ashes and charred wood.

The *regularly laid* pavement of flint nodules at Knook Barrow formed a triangular or trapezoidal area of 4.5m by 1.8m, 'narrowing as it approached the east end'. Like others it was covered with charred wood and burnt bones, both animal and human. Other local materials were sometimes used, chalk blocks at Arn Hill, on which the bones of three individuals had been placed and 'burr stones', which had been brought some distance from the Greensand, at King Barrow.

INTERNAL MOUNDS

At Wor Barrow, the skeletal material lay directly on the old ground surface between two small pits and was covered by a mound of turf which rose to 0.6m in height. Pitt Rivers depicted it as circular in the wooden model that he made of the excavated site (now in Salisbury Museum) and scaled up it would probably have been about 8.5m in diameter. Similarly, Cunnington wrote confidently of mounded deposits covering burials on Salisbury Plain. At the east end of Heytesbury North Field long barrow was a circular mound of black earth, flint nodules, chalk and some sarsen boulders, a number of which fell and made progress difficult. Within King Barrow, there was a circular mound of clay and earth. At the east end of Old Ditch, the deposits, evidently of chalk and turf, had the appearance of a conical mound, 'as though there had existed a circular barrow prior to the erection of the long barrow'. Others, in contrast, were ridged. Within Corton long barrow, there was a massive ridged cairn of flints and chalk measuring some 6 x 3m and reaching 2m in height. Surmounting it was a massive, probably sarsen, boulder 'that required three men to lift it out'. The deposit in Boles Barrow was similar. A considerable pile of stones (sarsen) and flints (nodules) was placed over the pavement narrowing to a central ridge at a height of 1.8m above the burials. Cunnington described it as 'like the ridge of a

42 Photograph of the cairn covering the bone deposits at the east end of Fussell's Lodge long barrow. *Courtesy of Paul Ashbee*

house'. At Knook, a ridge of flints and 'large man made stones' 1.3m high, sealed the pavement. The 'man made stones' are almost certainly sarsen, aside from flint the only naturally occurring stone in the vicinity and probably deliberately broken up into manageable pieces. At Arn Hill, a pile of 'large loose stones' laid over the pavement was probably also sarsen, perhaps similar to the cairn at Fussell's Lodge (*42*).

There appear to be two distinct traditions, one of circular mounds, the other (sub-) rectangular and ridged, although the reason for the difference is unclear. The external form of the barrows provides no indication of whether circular or ridged mounds might be concealed. Those excavated by Cunnington on Salisbury Plain all lie within a few miles of each other, yet both circular and ridged mounds are present, sometimes in adjacent mounds.

FAÇADE

At the easternmost end of Skendleby 1, a crescentic trench was set transversely to the axis with its concave side facing away from the monument. It was thought to be a bedding trench for a line of posts. Impressions indicated that these would have been large tree trunks of over 0.5m in diameter split in half and set closely together with the flat side towards the monument. There was no indication of height, but it must have been considerable as they were set to a depth of over 1.2m and were thought to have supported the material of the barrow mound to a height of almost a metre.

A façade at Skendleby 2 (*36*) began as a simple straight trench just under 13m in length, aligned towards the north-east. Varying a little either side of 1m in width and cut to a depth of around 1m, the trench had supported a wooden fence comprising at least 31 uprights probably linked together by horizontal panels or wattle. Given the maximum 0.4m diameter of the uprights, a fence height either side of about 3m can be postulated. At either end, a shallower, subsidiary trench was set at a 45° angle, in plan view giving the impression of a horned feature and although of lesser prominence, this also appears to have held fencing. At some point, the fence was burnt down and little evidence of it can have remained above ground. Dates of 3670-3340 cal. BC and 3360-3030 cal. BC at 95 per cent probability were obtained from the charcoal. The radiocarbon evidence indicates that one of the earliest features on site was the façade, which may have predated by some considerable time any burial deposit or mound construction.

The timbers of the façade had also been burnt at Willerby Wold, where a 12m long, slightly concave bedding trench, almost horn-like in plan, held a series of posts that were placed progressively deeper towards the centre where, at 1.1m deep, they may have been placed over a 'ritual pit'. The post setting here was thought to provide the eastern limit of a trapezoidal ditched mortuary enclosure, although as the latter seems to butt onto it, the contemporaneity of façade and enclosure is not absolutely clear.

Similar trenches have come from cairn sites. At Street House, Loftus, Cleveland, a trench 9m long by between 1.5 and 2m wide was cut to a depth of 0.8m with extensions set at oblique angles at either end to form a horned arrangement. It held a series of closely set posts of considerable size that must have formed a palisade-like feature. The excavator pointed out that the area would feel almost enclosed by posts creating an 'auditorium' (Vyner 1984). Like that at Willerby Wold, the post at the centre of the feature was set in a deeper pit than the rest and at 1m, had a greater diameter than the others. Indeed, the excavator discussed the difficulty of burning down such a post and suggested that it may have been hollow. It also lay in alignment with two other pits of similar size situated at right angles to it, which were thought to form elements of a mortuary structure. If so, the palisade must have been added to an existing post that formed part of an earlier structure and the radiocarbon dates appear to support this. Statistically combined radiocarbon dates provide slightly earlier date ranges for the mortuary structure (3653-3355 cal. BC) than for the façade trench (3515-3050 cal. BC).

With this in mind it may be worth turning to the façade trench at Fussell's Lodge (43). Here a bedding trench, 0.8m wide by 1.5m deep, left a small gap or causeway through it at the centre where a pit had been dug (Ashbee 1966, 6-8). The palisade trench had held massive posts leaving an entrance gap across which the pit 1.5 x 0.9 x 0.9m deep was subsequently cut. However, since the pit would have overlapped with the bedding trench on either side this would have been a difficult or impossible task if the posts were all in place. It seems possible that, it once held an upright forming part of a mortuary structure, subsequently removed to allow entrance when the façade was constructed. If so it would have formed an axial arrangement with two other pits of similar size that were considered to form elements of a burial chamber. Alternatively, the deep pits at the centre of the façade here may have had other origins and functions. Vyner's suggestion of a hollow trunk is original and in view of the inverted tree bole at Sea Henge, it is unnecessary to think it terms of neatly cut timbers.

At Haddenham, a 12m long façade comprising at least nine upright posts lay to the north-east of a wooden mortuary structure thought to be contemporary with it; their position being identified by impressions in the façade trench. The plan suggests that there may have been some reorganisation immediately in front of the structure, where a large circular impression as wide as the chamber had been surmounted by remnants of the façade posts (Hodder and Shand 1988). The feature has similarities with that at Fussell's Lodge. The feature at the centre of these facades, whether pit, post, or indeed tree hole, appear central to some of the structural activities, providing an integral link with the mortuary area.

FORECOURTS

The presence of a façade at the easternmost end tends to focus attention on that part of the structure. For about 1m on the outer side of the facade at Skendleby 1, the chalk ground surface had been lowered by almost 0.5m. The area was filled with what appears to have been midden material containing an abundance of small Neolithic potsherds and carbonised material, which spilled over into the façade bedding trench. Why such material should be placed at that point is unclear, but there are other indications that the area was of particular importance.

43 Photograph of the façade trench at Fussell's Lodge long barrow. *Courtesy of Paul Ashbee*

At Haddenham, a gravelled 'negative feature' extended for a distance of 5.5m from the façade. Into it, a post and panel fence had been set parallel to the façade but funnelling towards the mortuary structure. Gravel was placed between the façade and the fence forming a shallow bank up to about 1.5 wide. Such features may have provided a focal point and supported activities outside the façade; the group of five postholes at the easternmost end at Fussell's Lodge that channel activity towards the central feature of the facade and interpreted as a porch in front of the entrance, might also be considered in this way.

The rectangular structure located at right angles to the east of the mortuary area at Nutbane, Hampshire (*44*), was altogether more substantial. It comprised a discontinuous bedding trench over an area of just less than 6 x 5.5m. The side adjacent to the mortuary structure had a gap at both ends and this supported a series of posts spaced at 0.6 to 1.2m intervals. There were three large postholes situated along the centre of the rectangle. Two phases of use were postulated. First, was a construction of a slightly trapezoidal structure, 4.8 x 4.2m based on

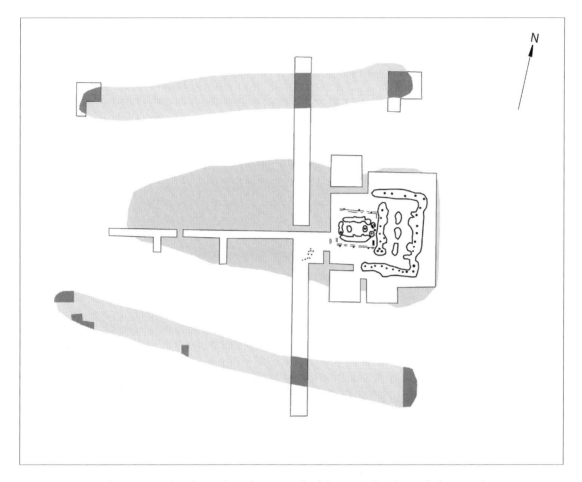

N

44 At Nutbane, excavation focused on the east end of the mound and revealed a complex arrangement of postholes and bedding trenches representing more than one phase of activity. *Redrawn from Morgan 1959*

four corner pits, three of which provided evidence that they had supported posts. These were deeper than the others, but strangely were thought to have supported smaller timbers. Following this, a slightly larger 7 x 4m rectangular structure was constructed. The material filling the structure contained evidence for burning and was markedly different from the finer chalk outside and this led the excavator to conclude that the posts must have supported log or plank walls. The central postholes were drawn in to the interpretation enabling postulation of a ridged roof, although the posts in the remainder of the bedding trench to the north and south of the building were interpreted as free-standing (*colour plate 17*). Other interpretations might be possible, particularly as the eastern and continuous part of the bedding trench has the look of a façade about it. Some of the posts in it were set at a 15° angle rather than upright and might have been problematical as roof supports. It could be that the whole structure was free-standing.

WOODEN MORTUARY STRUCTURES

In the literature, the terms burial chamber, mortuary chamber and mortuary enclosure are often used interchangeably. In some cases these are hardly chambers and some may not have been roofed. To avoid confusion the term mortuary structure is used here for an enclosed box-like feature that invariably contains skeletal remains often placed at the easternmost limit of the long barrow. Mortuary enclosures are larger areas and may not contain skeletal material. Thus the 'mortuary enclosure' referred to in the Nutbane report, is in fact a small, almost square structure 7 x 5.5m built of wooden uprights and horizontally laid logs. It had three posts in the north, five on the south and three in the east and as the horizontals continued beyond the verticals it was evidently not a jointed structure. It was seen as being linked to phase two of the forecourt structure, but was evidently later than the primary burials, although a further, potentially contemporary burial was subsequently inserted. This might also bear re-interpretation as the structure is strikingly similar to some of the bayed structures found in other mounds. Unfortunately Faith Morgan (nee Vatcher) did not investigate the mound further to the west, but there are slight indications in the published plan that the arrangement might have continued in either direction. Underlying the wooden structure was a system of discontinuous ditches forming a rectangle around the burials, not unlike the arrangement at New Wintles Farm, Oxfordshire (Kenward 1982), or the ditches of a diminutive barrow. The spoil was placed outside the ditches leaving the interior for three burials flanked by two large posts.

At Haddenham, a long barrow covered by anaerobic peat and clay allowed preservation of organic matter, specifically, a wooden structure (Hodder and Shand 1988). It consisted of considerable portions of the walls of a rectangular or slightly trapezoidal box-like construction, 7m in length and 1.3-1.6m wide, divided laterally by a plank into two separate cells, each just over 4m long (45). The walls comprise planking from split timbers, each c.1.3m wide and c.4m in length held in a vertical position internally by three vertical axial posts and revetted externally by a clay bank. The uprights, of 0.5-1.3m in diameter were of considerable size in relation to the structure and would have seriously impeded access. The structure was covered by a wooden roof, which is thought to have been flat, with planks resting on the uprights in a similar manner to chambers that are built in stone. A Grimston ware bowl and leaf-shaped arrowheads were found in association with the structure.

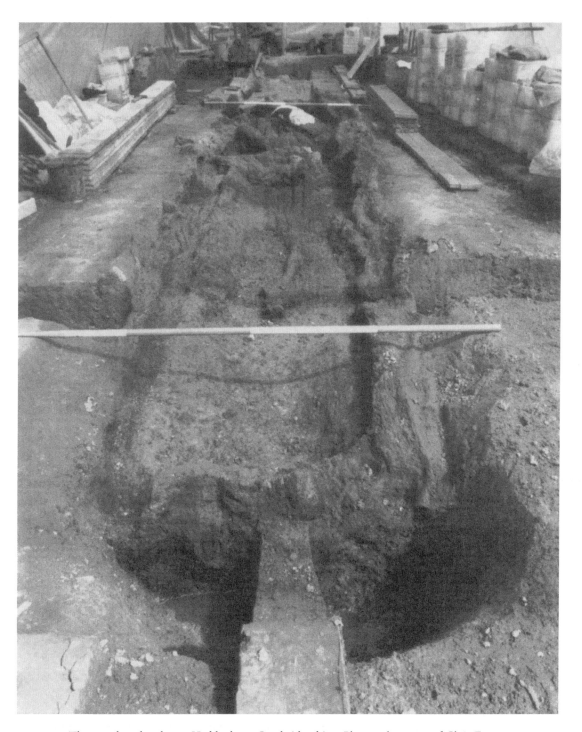

45 The wooden chamber at Haddenham, Cambridgeshire. *Photograph courtesy of Chris Evans*

CELL DIVISION, STALLS OR BAYS

Increasingly fenced divisions have been recognised as an integral part of mound construction. A spine of posts or stakes defined the axis of the monument at Skendleby 1 and supported a fence (46). Traces of uprights around 1m apart were found preserved within the mound to a height of 1m and fences were made by laying horizontal rods between them. Additional fences were set at right angles from the spinal posts, to form a series of cells or bays. According to the excavator they were set within the original topsoil and not driven into the underlying chalk to ensure stability. Along the sides of the structure was a series of small postholes set at an average distance apart of 1.5m. Like those in the central spine they were not anchored to the subsoil. Evidently the structure was not primarily designed to take weight and it was the division that was more important. Neither does it seem to have been designed specifically to retain soil, for the horizontal rods were set at c.40mm intervals through which it could easily filter. While the position of most spinal posts could be assigned a partner on the periphery, there were some that did not match, though it may be that there were unrecognised subdivisions. At no point did the cross-divisions reach the side posts, but the latter may have provided a marker and since there were no bays recorded on the north side of the spine, the side posts there need not have had such a relationship. One cell appears to have been constructed over the 'ritual' pit, the stakes cutting into its filling. Here the cell had been filled with loam, evidently in two phases, separated by a deposit of black midden material containing potsherds and flints. However, material in adjacent cells differed in composition; that to the south-west was in large part filled with chalk rubble, as was the opposite side of the spine at this point. Some bays contained clean, fine, chalk rubble that had set hard and become concrete-like, while others contained an admixture of earth (Philips 1936).

A similar system of bays was recorded at Skendleby 2, although here it appears to have overlaid both mortuary structure and remnants of a burnt façade and a number of small changes in its alignment were detected notably on either side of the façade and burial area. There were thought to be about 48 bays, each with an average width of 2.3m, but there was no lateral fence as at Skendleby 1, instead a revetment of chalk blocks. Filling of the bays was done in an orderly fashion – earth along the central axis, with periglacial material placed over that, all sealed by coarse chalk rubble, but construction was nevertheless considered to have been carried out in a piecemeal manner. In general, the central fence was aligned to the south-east, crossing the burial area at right angles and, was it not for a slight change in direction, would have crossed the façade slightly askew. There was some care to incorporate both the old façade and burial area within a single feature.

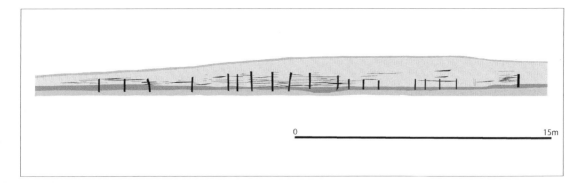

0   15m

46 Long section of the Giants Hills 1, Skendleby, long barrow (*redrawn from Philips 1936*) showing the arrangement of bays that may have originally extended for the full length of the mound

At South Street long barrow, the axial fence of stake holes (*47*), each 10cm in diameter, was oriented to the south-east and recorded for a length of just over 37m, with two minor and almost imperceptible changes of alignment. The cells, or bays, formed of slighter smaller diameter stakes, were about 1.8m wide but there was variation, from *c.*1m to above 2m, amounting to forty bays in total, although one or two may have been subdivided. Sometimes they were opposite one another, but this was not universally the case. The fence arrangement incorporated a group of five, apparently deliberately positioned, large sarsen boulders, three of which had been broken and placed on the turf of the old ground surface towards the south-east end. While the axial fence curved northwards to avoid one stone, an offset stake had also been removed to accommodate it. Placing of the stones was therefore seen as integrally related to, and contemporary with, the construction of the fence.

Each bay was filled with material thought to have derived from the side ditches, in a similar manner to Skendleby 2. It was placed in a regular order according to the manner in which the ditch would have been dug. Thus turf was piled against the central fence essentially forming a central axial turf stack: against that was chalky soil, then coombe rock and finally chalk. There were, however, a considerable number of irregularities. South of the axial fence, one bay had a smaller turf stack, another had 22 small sarsen boulders placed against the axial fence, a third, an unusually thin bay had no turf, while the extra width of the adjacent bay compensated for it. Two others had a reduced quantity of turf, one had none at all, and two others contained small sarsen boulders. No artefacts were encountered that were directly associated with the structure, but four cattle scapulae and six fragments of red deer antler, probably tools used in extraction of materials from the ditch, were found in the chalk rubble or coombe rock layers.

47 Reconstruction of some of the fenced bays at South Street. The uprights were subsequently joined by horizontal hurdling. *Photograph courtesy of the Alexander Keiller Museum, Avebury*

These cellular features were also present at Beckhampton Road, where the axial fence, oriented to the north-east, was traced for 28m and comprised 59 stake holes. Again offset fences were placed at right angles in this case forming at least 20 cells or bays and again a lateral fence, situated along the perimeter secured the outer edge and was revetted by a dump of chalk gravel. In some instances sharp divisions distinguished in the nature of the filling might indicate the presence of bays even though stake holes were not recognised. Indeed there were examples of planking in two instances. If these are included, the number of bays may approach the total at South Street. Here, the infilling of each bay, was more varied than at South Street. Most cells incorporated a few turves, but three had turf stacks. South of the axial fence, two bays were filled with coombe rock and some chalk marl and another with mixed coombe rock and chalk gravel. Others contained brickearth. Small sarsens were placed against fences in four bays and the excavator thought that they may have been used as hammers for the stakes. Toward the tail end of the structure, stacks of turves formed cell-like arrangements even where the fencing could not be traced. Such vertical stacks and breaks in the stratigraphy have been use to suggest that bays were present in others mounds but unrecognised at the time of excavation, at Thickthorn Down, for example (Bradley and Entwistle 1985).

There was no sign of burials in either of the Avebury mounds, nor was there mortuary structure or enclosure. The animal bones at South Street were all small and fragmentary and any number may have derived from the materials ripped up with turf from the old ground surface above the ditch. At Beckhampton Road it was a similar story. Three cattle skulls were found well separated but each relatively close to the central axis. One on the ground surface at the proximal end in the first bay facing the end of the mound (domestic ox), a second placed more centrally and the other at the distal end in a bay-like deposit of chalk gravel. More antler tools were found; at least 10 picks and 2 rakes, as well as other pieces and fragments. Most came from the mound make up, but there were two placed arrangements on the ground surface. In one, a rake had been placed on top of two picks. In the other, two picks were placed 'one above the other'.

Similar arrangements of infill have been noted at long cairns in the Cotswolds. At Hazleton North, Alan Saville recorded 16 cellular units in the construction of the mound situated either side of an axial line (Saville 1990), although here it was considered to be an expedient constructional device to bind the cairn together. The arrangement also recalls the Orkney stalled cairns which had from 7-14 bays. The Knowe of Ramsey, for example, had 14 compartments, while at Midhowe, protruding slabs of stone created 12 divisions, with stone benches along one side most of which contained burials (Davidson and Henshall 1989, 135-148). A similar process can also be recognised further afield; Madsen (1979) for example, depicted cell arrangements in mounds at Barkae and Østergård in Denmark. The lack of burials at South Street and Beckhampton, coupled with the widespread use suggests that it was more than a construction technique and that it may have been central to the ideas and purpose of creating barrows.

MORTUARY ENCLOSURES

Excavations at both Wor Barrow and Fussell's Lodge demonstrated that long mortuary enclosures were an integral part of some long barrows. Both comprised an arrangement of palisade-like timbers, with posts closely set within a bedding trench. The Fussell's Lodge example was trapezoidal in plan, formed by a ditch 35m long and 8.2m at the widest end reducing to 5.5m, that butted on to the façade trench; very similar in form to that at Willerby Wold. Curiously, both had an oblique distal end. In contrast, the version at Wor Barrow was rectangular, similar to the example beneath Kilham long barrow. In both cases, an opening in the palisade at the easternmost end, or at Wor Barrow a constriction of the trench, produced a porch-like feature suggesting that it might mark an entrance.

In both cases, however, the mound covering the burials would have all but blocked access once they had been built. If the shape of the enclosure was of importance, then the space must have been used in some way and one is left to assume that the burials and their covering may have been part of a blocking procedure. Excavations elsewhere, at sites not covered by mounds, for example, Rivenhall, Essex (Buckley *et al.* 1988), or Raunds, Northamptonshire (Windell *et al.* 1990), have produced little evidence from the interior to assist with the problem of function. At Raunds there were just two tree hollows within the enclosure. Only at North Stoke, Oxfordshire, where Humphrey Case excavated the terminal of an enclosure that had been largely destroyed by quarrying was a contemporary feature, a single posthole.

CREMATORIA

Several sites, predominantly, but not exclusively in Yorkshire, contain an area where bones have been burnt by creating excessive temperatures in an enclosed space. This is distinct from episodes of burning on open fires or cremation pyres, or the burning of façades. Terry Manby suggested that at Willerby Wold, the crematorium comprised flanking banks of turf, earth and chalk, similar to the embanked arrangement at Nutbane, between which human bones were placed. Over this, blocks of chalk and flint mixed with timber were placed, forming a ridged structure. The mound was then covered with turf and earth and finally given a capping of chalk rubble which covered the ditches of both mortuary enclosure and the area of the dismantled façade. William Greenwell was the first to suggest that some of these features were designed to create a draught in order to create high temperatures and produce a kiln-like effect. At Kill Barrow, Wiltshire, the heat had been so intense that it had fused chalk and bone, staining some of it blue in the process and forming what Thurnam described as 'ossiferous breccia' (*colour plate 18*).

Many of the features, fences, palisade-like constructions, piles of turf and soil imply a close link with the land. Numbers of trees were cut down and moved for building purposes, withies gathered, perhaps from managed hazel coppices, earth dug from one place and put in another. They tell us something of the landscape and land-use as well. The barrows were close to formerly cultivated areas. Whether the move from agriculture to grazing noted from evidence beneath some barrows was part of a cycle or imposed by other factors, climatic, social or economic is unknown. This wider context, however, is intriguing and worth considering whether further information can be extracted about the nature of these mounds.

5

LONG BARROWS AND THE LAND

NATIONAL DISTRIBUTION

Long barrows are widely distributed across Britain from the north of Scotland to Cornwall. The focus of the known concentration of earthen examples, however, occurs around the higher ground of central Wessex: Wiltshire, Hampshire, Dorset, West Sussex and in the north, Yorkshire and Lincolnshire (*48* and *49*). On closer inspection they predominantly occupy the chalk and limestone areas of those counties, places that until recently were considered largely marginal in agricultural terms and often turned over to sheep farming. The Wiltshire chalk, for example, sustained huge numbers of sheep during the historic period, which had the effect of ensuring the widespread preservation of monuments.

Passing through, Daniel Defoe (1724) commented on how vast the great flocks on the downs were, but he also mentioned that large areas were being gradually turned over to cultivation. Widespread agricultural inroads were made into these regions in the eighteenth and nineteenth centuries following Inclosure, leaving the Reverend A.C. Smith of Yatesbury, near Avebury, to record the monuments from horseback before the advances of agriculture could level them (Smith 1884). Even then the parish of Upavon could support a flock of over 3000.

During the twentieth century archaeological research focused heavily on the downland, as the discipline proved only too keen to investigate the dramatic monuments and this work, in turn, provided only more evidence of a chalk based concentration. Historically, even aerial photography followed the same pattern, investigating the chalk because, drawn by the presence of monuments, that is where new finds might be expected.

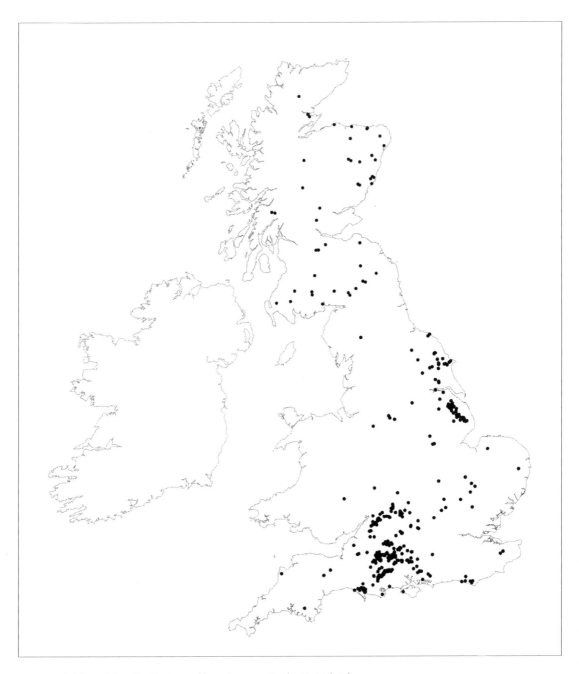

48 Map of the distribution of long barrows in the British Isles

49 Map of the distribution of long mortuary enclosures in British Isles

In contrast, much if not most of the lower ground had been cultivated long before, particularly that closer to favoured settlement locations by streams and rivers – areas more conducive to early agriculture. Chris Taylor (1972) named these areas the *zone of destruction*, where productive soils had encouraged cultivation and where such activities had from early historic times levelled any traces of previous activity.

In the final years of the twentieth century, however, new trends appeared. In particular, aerial photography began discovering great numbers of ring ditches along river valleys and Peter Woodward (1978) was able to suggest that the great clusters in the Ouse valley in Northamptonshire were mostly levelled round barrows. Aerial survey plots now make it clear that there are almost as many round barrows on Thanet in Kent as around Stonehenge (RCHME 1989) and there is scarcely a 1:10,000 scale map sheet of English Heritage's National Mapping Programme that doesn't contain at least one ring ditch.

Increasingly, the same can be said for long barrows. Including long mortuary enclosures, a survey of cropmarks in Kent identified twelve new sites in 1989 and undoubtedly many more remain to be discovered (*49*). The clues were perhaps always there. In 1936, Stuart Piggott excavated a long mound on the slopes of the river terrace gravel of the Stour Valley at Holdenhurst, near Christchurch, in Hampshire (Piggott 1937a). Considerably reduced, it survived to a mere 1.2m in height and was fortunately discovered and excavated before the expansion of the Bournemouth conurbation could erase it.

Flights along river valleys continue to reveal the presence of ring ditches and long enclosures. A single sortie along the middle reaches of the River Avon discovered three new cemeteries of round and oval barrows, in the case of Downton providing greater context for the Giant's Grave long barrow, situated a little further upslope (*50*). At Damerham, at the head of a tributary of the Avon, the discovery of a cemetery of ring ditches included a new long barrow with side ditches and a second, smaller 'Cranborne Chase' style long barrow nearby. Ten kilometres upstream and set within a re-entrant lies another site, Fussell's Lodge, almost plough-levelled when excavated by Paul Ashbee in the 1950s. Gradually new discoveries are providing links between Holdenhurst on the coast and well-known sites in the hinterland. The concentration of sites reflects both historic land-use and archaeological responses to it. The original distribution was not restricted to the chalk and limestone and it is a primary research aim to discover its true extent.

The riverine focus is widespread. Further upstream around Amesbury the pattern continues with long barrows situated on or close to the bluff or upper slope on either side of the valley. Aerial photography has made a contribution here too, recording the presence of examples at Netheravon Bake and in similar locations near Woodhenge, at Ablington and Milston northwards alongside the Avon (*colour plate 19*). The position of a further example, Sheer Barrow, almost

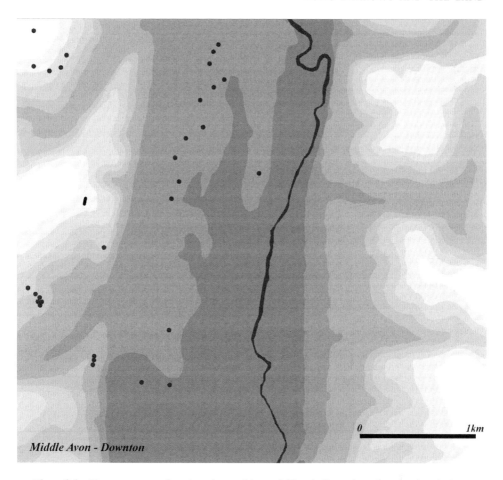

Middle Avon - Downton

0 _____ 1km

50 Plot of the Downton area showing the position of Giant's Grave long barrow in relation to the topography and later round barrows

levelled within the village arable at Figheldean Field was confirmed by geophysical survey (*30*). The situation is paralleled by that along the upper reaches of the River Wylye, a tributary of the River Avon that rises around Warminster and has its confluence at Salisbury. In its upper reaches, a series of five long barrows appear to focus on the river valley. Some, like Stockton, Corton or Boyton lie on the upper slope or bluff, others are situated closer to the valley floor or like Sherrington adjacent to the river edge. An unnamed minor tributary of the Wylye lies to the north and, evidently once of greater significance, has carved out a sheltered, now almost hidden valley within the interior of Salisbury Plain Military Training Area. Long barrows flank this valley too: long known examples at Heytesbury North Field, Oxendean Down, Norton Bavant and Middleton Down, as well as an oval barrow situated within Scratchbury Hillfort.

A further group clusters around Tilshead, the source of the River Till. Three of them, Tilshead Lodge, White Barrow and Old Ditch are positioned on interfluves between narrow re-entrants that lead to the main valley, while Kill Barrow remains a little further distant. A single example from east of the Till, the appropriately named East Barrow, lies at the head of a long narrow coombe and forms part of the group.

Barrows on the North Wiltshire Downs, near Avebury, also focus on rivers and tributary streams, particularly those close to the River Kennet. The mounds at East and West Kennet are situated on interfluves above re-entrant coombes that feed into the main stream, while a barrow recently discovered from the air by Roger Featherstone is situated on the bluff of White Hill immediately above the 'valley of stones' at Lockeridge (*colour plate 20*). The Longstones long barrow (*colour plate 21*) lies parallel to and just 200m from the Beckhampton Stream at a point where it turns to the south, while Beckhampton Road lies in the same valley, although at a point where the stream now rarely carries water even in winter. To the north of Avebury, Mill Barrow in the fields of Winterbourne Monkton is less than 200m from the stream, while the Shelving Stones, a monument illustrated by John Aubrey and perhaps once part of a chambered long barrow, lay just a little further distant in a similar position on the opposite bank. Even those on the higher downland, Easton Down, Horton Down, Kitchen Barrow and Rough Ridge Barrow, lie adjacent to coombes with potential winterbourne springs. Today much water is taken from the chalk aquifer by the military and water companies and this has dramatically affected the level of the water table. Ordnance Survey maps as well as the Reverend A.C. Smith's nineteenth-century illustrations depict water in now dry coombes (Aldsworth 1973-4).

The long barrows in Cranborne Chase invariably focus on present or former springs. Heywood Sumner depicts this on his plan of the Oakley Down round barrow cemetery, where Wor Barrow is attendant, while Martin Green (2000) has demonstrated the presence of a former lake at the source of the River Allen which was still likely to have been present in the Neolithic. In Oxfordshire, the Lambourn long barrow on Westcott Down marked the springs of the Lambourn stream and provided subsequent focus for the Bronze Age Seven Barrows cemetery that included bell and disc types.

Water with its life giving and cleansing powers is often considered of spiritual importance and across the world such places often have supernatural significance (Snead and Preucel 1999: essays in Carmichael 1994). Springs, in particular, provide an interface with the inner earth and as they also serve a practical role, they can be particularly effective at transmitting social memory (Crumley 1999). They help to anchor cosmologies, being at one end of the river, notably the end where it is 'born' and provide a backsight to assist with orientation (Theodoratus and Lapena 1994).

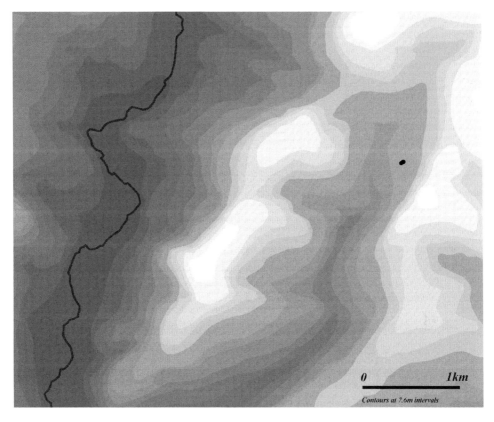

51 Plot of the Fussell's Lodge area showing the relationship of the mound to the local topography

Towards the source of watercourses many of the valleys become extremely narrow. Activities that might take place on the wider valley floor further downstream are thus forced onto the flanks. This might account for the siting of some monuments such as Kill Barrow, or those situated on interfluves between narrow valleys around Tilshead. It might also explain the location of a number of sites on Cranborne Chase, where long barrows are located on the ridges alongside the upper reaches of tributary streams.

Many barrows occupy the low ground, either by being located immediately adjacent to rivers or streams or in the sense of being dwarfed by the surrounding landscape. The wider picture continuously emphasises the use of river basins, with the extant examples surviving in the upper reaches. There are obvious examples such as Sherrington, constructed on the lip of the river edge: the Raunds long mounds adjacent to the River Nene, Jullieberrie's Grave adjacent to the River Stour and the long barrow at Foulmire Fen, Haddenham, which is situated on a shallow elevation alongside the River Ouse (Hodder and Shand 1988, 349).

Others occupy low positions beneath hill slopes, the barrows at Milston (*26*) are located at the foot of Beacon Hill, Wiltshire, while Fussell's Lodge long barrow, discovered from the air in 1924 (Crawford and Keiller 1928), lay enclosed within a re-entrant valley, surrounded on three sides by rising chalk hills which give the impression of a natural henge-like arena (*51*).

In Kent, survivals are located along the Medway and Stour at the point where the rivers begin to make their way through the chalk while at the opposite end of the country the trapezoidal mound at Dalladies, Fettercairn and the barrow at Capo just over 1km away both lay on the gravel terrace of the River North Esk in north-east Scotland (Collier *et al.* 2002). Long mortuary enclosures were constructed in similar positions; for example, one was discovered at Churton in Cheshire, overlooking the flood plain of the River Dee (Morgan V. and P. 2004, 38), while others such as Rivenhall in Essex (Buckley *et al.* 1988) and Dorchester in Oxfordshire (Atkinson *et al.* 1951) conform to the pattern.

In Sussex, Money Burgh and Cliffe Hill flank the River Ouse, while Alfriston, Long Burgh, Hunters Burgh, Exceat and possibly Windover Hill line the Cuckmere valley as they pass through the chalk. Much of the Sussex coastline has been eroded by the sea since the Neolithic, however, and further barrows may have been lost. The tell-tale diverging side ditches of a long barrow were rediscovered from the air by Roger Featherstone flying for the RCHME little more than 300m from the cliff edge on the golf course at Rottingdean. This is almost certainly the mound noted by Turner (1863, 243-4) as 'removed' in 1883 to level a cricket pitch, during which four adult skeletons and a small burial urn were found.

The great mounds of Lincolnshire occur on the Wolds, principally at the southern end. Here erosion has created steep sided narrow valleys similar to many on the southern chalk. At Skendleby, two long mounds known as the Giant's Hills flank the upper reaches of an unnamed tributary of the River Lymn (*52*). Both lie parallel to it on the upper slopes of the hillside, though below the summit, and both are invisible from the Roman road, little more than 200m away that follows the top of the ridge. Two further monuments, a long mortuary enclosure and a spoon-shaped enclosure were recently recorded from the air to the north-west of Skendleby 1 (*53*). A mound at Spellow Hills (*colour plate 22*) occupies a similar location at the head of a valley, although it is unusual in that it is aligned across the contours facing down slope. Two long mounds known as Deadman's Graves occupy an almost identical location in a narrow steep sided valley to the north. Again the mounds here lie below the highest ground and their position is intimately linked to the valley itself, beyond which they are invisible.

Some valley slopes are very much steeper than others, particularly in upstream areas where courses cut deeper into bedrock. Others created by Eocene and Pliocene sea transgressions have left broader basins with dramatic sides. Thus

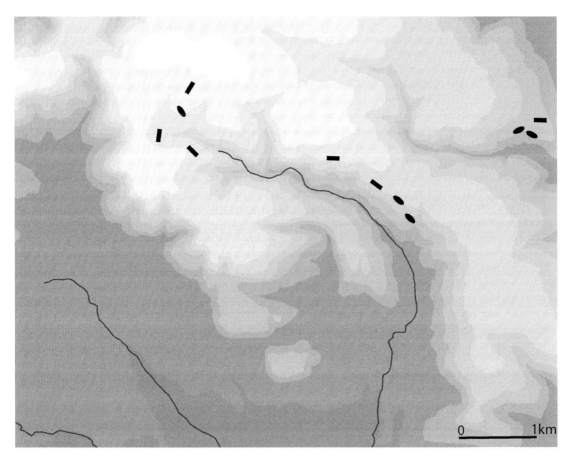

52 Plot of the Skendleby area showing the extant long barrows (ovals) in relation to the topography. Deadman's Grave 1 and 2 (upper right) have now been joined by an ovoid enclosure recorded on air photographs, while the Giants Hills barrows 1 and 2 are now joined by a long mortuary enclosure and a 'spoon-shaped' enclosure at the same elevation, while the single mound at Spellow Hills has three adjacent long mortuary enclosures all recorded from air photographs

some barrows are found on the lip of escarpment edges. These are often on what has become known as the false crest, the first high point to be visible from a valley when ascending a slope and below the ultimate summit (54). Such barrows are often not visible from positions at the base of the escarpment, but can be seen from locations in the middle distance. Given the length of such escarpments one might expect to find great numbers of barrows ranged along them, but such sitings are relatively rare. Along a 30km stretch of the northern escarpment of Salisbury Plain only Arn Hill, Bratton, Edington, and Giant's Grave at Pewsey are known. Along the northern escarpment of Pewsey

53 Air photograph of mortuary enclosure or levelled long barrow at Ulceby, Lincolnshire (NMR 17822-21). This is part of the Giant's Hills group where four long barrows and enclosures, two each either side of the Ulceby/Skendleby parish boundary, are situated almost side by side and line the slope of the valley above a small stream for almost a kilometre. This spoon-shaped enclosure is broken by a quarry (covered by trees in the centre of the picture) in which Dilwyn Jones carried out some small-scale excavation in 1989-90. A red deer antler recovered from the primary silt of the northernmost ditch produced a radiocarbon date range of 3635-3340 cal. BC BM-2750 (Jones D. 1998). © *English Heritage NMR*

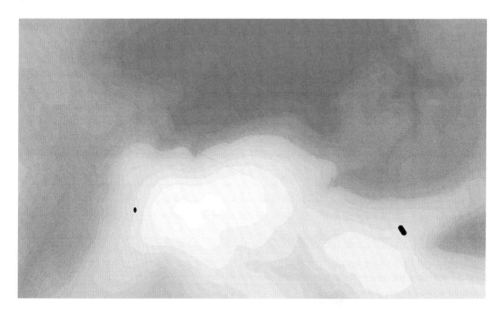

54 Plot of the Tidcombe area, showing the location of Tidcombe long mound (right) and Tow Barrow (left) in relation to the local topography. Neither takes the highest ground, instead being placed on the upper slopes overlooking the valley

Vale, the focus of many chance finds of Neolithic axes, only Adam's Grave, is prominently visible (*colour plate 23*). Along the east facing middle and lower escarpments of the North Wiltshire Downs there are none. Along the 25km stretch of escarpment overlooking the Vale of the White Horse above the Upper Thames valley, Wayland's Smithy and a long barrow near Uffington Castle are the only long barrows present. Despite the number of round barrows situated along the summit of the South Downs escarpment overlooking the Weald, no long barrows occur. Neither are there any in such positions on the North Downs. Generally the *highest points* in the landscape were avoided, both in terms of prominent hills such as Sidbury Hill or Beacon Hill on Salisbury Plain, the Hogs Back in Surrey, or broad interfluves. Rather than being placed on Tan Hill, the most striking point of the Marlborough Downs, barrows are positioned at lower elevations to the west and north. It might be argued that such high places were irrelevant to local people or it might be that they were considered too sacred to defile by constructing monuments on them.

Dramatic and prominent locations are not therefore an essential ingredient in the siting of long barrows. There are, however, some high-level barrows that appear to break the rules. In the centre of Salisbury Plain, Ell Barrow, Boles Barrow and Knighton Barrow, all extremely large examples, are located on broad high positions and visible in all directions for considerable distances. They are large dramatic monuments, particularly Knighton and Ell Barrow which are of great bulk. Where barrows occur on escarpment edges, the prominent siting means that they can be seen for considerable distances in a certain direction; however, approached from the opposite direction, the dip slope, they are sometimes hardly visible at all. Thoughtful siting a few metres away would have ensured greater all round visibility. On Portsdown, the dramatic escarpment above the coastal plain at Portsmouth, two and possibly three long barrows are situated on the lip of the scarp, from where they could be seen from far out to sea. They are particularly visible across the coastal plain below where one might expect settlement to be located, placement some metres to the north would have ensured far greater all round visibility.

Given suggestions of the significance of the sea in barrow location (Tilley 1994), at just 3km from the *present* coastline much could be made of the Holdenhurst location and it might be expected that a sea-view could have been important. Although now difficult to check with precision in the field because of the presence of a housing estate (55), observation of the contours suggests the sea was obscured from view and could not have been a primary factor in location of the monument, for placing it just a few metres to the south would have provided a perfect view. Instead, it is intimately linked to the lower ground to the north, the Stour Valley and perhaps its tributary the Moors River.

55 While the location of Holdenhurst long barrow is reflected in the road name there is no other sign of it. Located on the valley slope it focused on the River Stour to the north rather than the coastal plain to the south

The greater chance of survival on the higher ground has led to suggestions of barrows being located according to some rule of intervisibility. Isobel Smith indicated that the most frequent situation in Hampshire was that in which the monument occupied the skyline when viewed from below (RCHME 1979a), but while a monument might be so placed where a good part of the local community could see it, that is rather different from designing intervisibility between long barrows. Any location higher than the surrounding ground will, intervening vegetation notwithstanding, be visible across a greater area than a site on the lower ground.

Although it is not universally the case, there are a considerable number of barrows that are located on the eastern slope of hills. West Kennet is on the eastern slope of a spur; East Kennet similarly, Pimperne is on the eastern side, although on an interfluve Thickthorn Down is placed east of the summit, Chettle is east, Wor Barrow east, as are the Vern Ditch Chase barrows (*colour plate 24*). Only rarely are barrows located on the western slopes, Jullieberrie's Grave in Kent is one. Pre-occupation with such places may have agricultural purpose.

In some places in the greatly rolling downland, within the deep coombes of Salisbury Plain and Dorset, the low winter sun rarely reaches the valley floor and such places can retain frost throughout much of the day. The asymmetrical chalk valleys themselves are a result of this, differential post-glacial melting of the surface according to which side of the valley received the greater amount of sunlight. Such east facing locations will often be less steep and naturally more advantageous for both cultivation and settlement. These factors may underpin any cosmological system based on solar or lunar alignments. Stonehenge and Durrington Walls are also set on eastern slopes and here Tim Darvill (1997) has suggested a cosmological scheme in which the east is associated with sunrise, birth, fertility, while the west is associated with sunset, darkness, cold and death.

RELATIONSHIP WITH CAUSEWAYED ENCLOSURES

The lengthy chronology of long barrow use allows considerable overlap with that of causewayed enclosures, although the relationship of the two monument types remains unclear. Long barrows were undoubtedly the earlier type to be introduced and might be expected to provide the architectural influence in terms of palisade or fence erection, ditch digging or bank construction. It may be that an early causewayed phase of ditch digging is unrecognised at some long barrows. Such constructional techniques were certainly well-understood by 3700-3600 cal. BC when the earlier causewayed enclosures began to appear. There are date ranges of around the beginning of the fourth millennium at Thickthorn Down for the buried soil (4040-4200 cal. BC, 4040-3900 or 3880-3800 cal. BC BM-2355), but date ranges for ditch digging events at Wor Barrow (3700-3000 cal. BC BM-2283R and 3800-3050 cal. BC BM-2284R) and Badshot Lea (3640-3550, 3540-3500 or 3430-3380 cal. BC BM-2273) are more comfortably associated with the causewayed enclosure period.

Realisation that skeletal material found in long barrows had often been retrieved from elsewhere, coupled with the finds of human bone at causewayed enclosures, led to suggestions that the enclosures had been used as excarnation centres and the bones collected and transferred to long barrows. No single barrow contains enough bones to cater for the population inferred in the construction of the embanked and ditched enclosures, although remains could have been spread around several such monuments in the vicinity. Many mounds, however, lie at considerable distance from any enclosure and undiscovered examples notwithstanding, it could be that the bones were collected from somewhere else altogether.

Two long barrows are located on Hambledon Hill, one of them small and inconspicuous and the other large, monumental and prominently sited. The larger occupies the ultimate summit of the hill, just outside the causewayed enclosure, but the smaller of the two lies between the earthen banks and ditches of the main enclosure and the southern cross-dykes of the Hanford Spur. The estimated date of the smaller long barrow at Hambledon is 3700–3500 cal. BC but centres on 3650 BC, just before the first phase of causewayed enclosure construction. The site was partly excavated in 1974 by Roger Mercer, who demonstrated that the causewayed enclosure earthworks were constructed over a period of three to four hundred years from c.3600–3300 cal. BC (Healy 2004) and, like Whitehawk (Ross Williamson 1930), Briar Hill (1985) and other sites, represent a lengthy period of intermittent development, with the earthworks being periodically re-cut and added to. The ditch of the small long barrow also underwent a number of phases of activity. A Cornish stone axe and pottery was placed in the ditch on the primary silt. The mound then appears to have gone out of use as a considerable quantity of its material weathered into the ditch. A small trench was subsequently cut in the ditch and flint, pottery and bone deposited, only to be backfilled and re-cut (Mercer 1980). The process ensured that the long barrow was fully incorporated into a cycle of renewal.

Horslip long barrow lies on the slopes beneath the Windmill Hill causewayed enclosure in Wiltshire, from where it is just visible, but it is of sufficient distance away to be unaffected by it. A small square enclosure, 10m across, to the east of the enclosure contained a dozen pits and a certain amount of pottery in the interior which attests to visits during several archaeological periods. None of it came from secure contexts but the site was considered to be a small mortuary enclosure (Smith 1965). A similar, though slightly larger site was excavated just 100m from the causewayed enclosure at Abindon, Oxfordshire, where the first phase of a rectangular enclosure, 15 x 12m, introduced a sequence of successive re-cuts subsequently covered by a small oval barrow (Bradley 1992).

Richard Bradley (1983) perceptively noted that the bank barrow at Maiden Castle changes orientation at either end of the central portion which stands alone as a more prominent earthwork and which at approximately 50m in length may in fact be a long barrow. In this case, the long barrow element is located just metres outside the causewayed enclosure perimeter. At Roughton, Norfolk, a site levelled by cultivation, one and possibly two long barrows lie within 100m of the causewayed enclosure (Oswald et al. 2001) and there are several long barrows within the vicinity of Robin Hood's Ball causewayed enclosure, although the closest of which, Figheldean 31, at 600m downslope, hardly influences it. In Sussex, an oval ring ditch, 2km distant from the Trundle, and probably an Abingdon or Cranborne Chase style long barrow, was excavated by Southern Archaeology, the first phase ditch containing Mortlake Ware, and a ground discoidal knife (Chichester Museum) was dated to 3040–2870 cal.

BC (Turner 1997: James Kenny pers. comm.). At Whitehawk, near Brighton in Sussex, a causewayed enclosure with at least six circuits of interrupted banks and ditches, an anomaly occurs in the course of the second circuit. In the north, the ditch makes an angled turn and while this may merely be a quirk of its layout, given the symmetry elsewhere on site, it seems more likely that it is designed to avoid or incorporate a pre-existing feature. According to Ross Williamson's excavation plan (1930, 60), the ditch curves around a bank terminal before being interrupted by a causeway. Curwen shows a length of bank to the north of this, adjacent to the ditch excavated in 1929. This is the only part of the second bank noted by him, so it must have been more prominent than the rest. Indeed, it is depicted on both plans as a long mound, measuring approximately 16m long and 9.5m wide. While smaller than most long barrows, aligned as it is east-south-east, it is nevertheless tempting to link it with that type of field monument.

It is less usual to find a long barrow *within* the causewayed enclosure. Only perhaps, at Crickley Hill, where a 100m-long shallow long mound lies within the enclosure, and is thought by the excavator to be late in the site sequence. It may have served a similar purpose to the bank barrow at Maiden Castle. More pertinently a small elongated arrangement of pits underlay the causewayed enclosure earthworks and within which there may have been a mound (Dixon 1988, 78). This was a mere 10 x 4m, recalling the early feature at Whitehawk.

While dating of these respective features is in most cases unknown, where there is some form of chronological relationship, and Abingdon aside, the long barrows appear to be earlier than the enclosures. In some cases they are incorporated into the arrangements, in others left narrowly outside. Construction of causewayed enclosures implies that the manner in which the barrows and the land around them were used changed. Ros Cleal's period of rapid change may have resulted in revised perceptions of such places.

6

MONUMENTS AND THE
SOCIAL LANDSCAPE

HAZELNUTS

Evidence of the longevity of use of some locations stretching back for millennia is provided at certain monuments. Sometimes this is simply an odd residual microlith incorporated in the mound make up. In others there appears to be more substantial evidence of Mesolithic activity on the old ground surface. None of this by itself should occasion any surprise, for we might expect large parts of the landscape to have been utilised in one way or another in the several millennia prior to monument construction. While the overall population may not have been large, towards the end of the Mesolithic there are indications that parts of the country were, relatively speaking, quite intensively used. Investigating the role of hazelnuts in the Mesolithic diet in Hampshire and the area needed to supply such needs, Roger Jacobi concluded that the whole of the land was utilised and there was little room for newcomers operating a different lifestyle. While the use of marine foods in the diet declined (Richards and Hedges 1999), the importance of hazelnuts continued well into the fourth millennium. They were present at lowland river side sites at, for example, Yarnton (Hey 1997, 109) and Eton Rowing Course (Allen *et al.* 2004) and formed an important component of the plant register at Whitesheet Hill causewayed enclosure in Wiltshire (Hinton in Rawlings *et al.* 2004, 177-9). Fragments of hazel were also found at Skendleby 1 (Cecil in Phillips 1936, 103-6) with carbonised nut shells east of the revetment trench and in the midden material overlying the pit.

We might expect all of the springs, rivulets, streams and rivers to have been fully exploited and the land around them incorporated into well-established subsistence patterns. Any deviance from the pattern, intervention from outside, that expropriated a hazelnut patch or fish resource could result in stress in the indigenous group and probably result in friction. Curating hazelnuts, vegetables, fruit, fish, let alone mammals can only have resulted over time in a conserved landscape with a population that occupied a certain well-defined territory where individuals could be certain of resource yield. Given the crucial role of water in stock management such resource units were, in all probability, based on drainage patterns and river frontage, much as Jordon (2001) has described for the Khanti of Siberia, with respective parts of the landscape reserved for hunting and gathering at certain times of the year.

It is true that there is little evidence for permanent dwellings or even flimsy structures at this time, but in part that may be the result of erosion and soil mechanics. The surface of the chalk has been truncated by at least 0.5m, enough to ensure that all but the most deeply anchored postholes do not survive, while the better settlement locations, those sheltered areas by rivers and streams will have suffered the results of fluvial processes, flood scouring and meander erosion. However, that such domestic structures did exist is demonstrated by the discovery of a hut at Howick, on the Northumberland coast that was rebuilt and periodically occupied for more than a century (Waddington 2003).

Such activities and occupation might result in the engraving of certain places on the land surface, scarring the countryside, trails out of settlements to nurtured gathering places, or as Isaac (1981) would put it, repeated trips to a favoured fruit tree, or places persistently visited as they were good for hunting or fowling (Barton et al. 1995), or a well-placed crag or rock good for observing game from behind. Places might be marked in other ways. The site of a particularly difficult or heroic aurochs kill where trees might be marked or decorated in memory or appreciation of the event as Ingold's (2000) ethnographic examples suggest. Such places and many others may have attained cultural status with memory and storytelling over time.

Some places were being marked in a monumental way as early as the eighth millennium. The three large pine posts erected adjacent to what later became Stonehenge (Cleal et al. 1995) may have been carved and decorated, or like Sea Henge might simply involve upturned trees, but whatever manifestation they took, it implies that the location was marked in a way that others were not. Considerable effort went into cutting down and erecting the posts, effectively changing the landscape, intervening in the natural order of things. How widespread such activities were is unknown, but knowledge of silviculture may have been inherent in a lifestyle influenced by wooded environments. It may even be that hazel was deliberately coppiced, effectively providing the rudiments on which later, use of the material, in for example, the Neolithic Sweet Track in Somerset, was based.

Now to approach the matter from another point of view, that of the Neolithic monument builder. In part, the invisibility of Neolithic settlement has resulted in the current view of a nomadic or semi-nomadic population returning periodically to places of ancestral importance marked by the barrows, causewayed enclosures and flint mines. It might thus be argued that the monuments were the products of regional groups denoting the presence of good pasture; alternatively that they mark the grazing rights of transhumant groups with their base camps elsewhere. Should several groups be present the problems are more considerable, as in terms of exploitation of resources it implies a free-for-all that is at odds with the order implied by the number of monuments. Pasture used by one nomadic group on its round cannot then be used by another, thus putting the health of the latter herd at risk. The same applies to fish stocks and other wild foods. However, the barrows at least in their final stages are monumental, some absolutely massive. All that is needed to mark such areas is a notice, a totem, a painting, a label and the mere fact that the land has been used and modified is enough to signify presence to others. But all of this takes no account of pre-existing land-use and it assumes a need to be constantly on the move that is more than resource led.

Alternatively it may be that each barrow marks the holding of a sedentary, perhaps extended family group. Given the UK climate and vegetation the parish-sized units around each barrow contain more than sufficient resources for quite large groups of people and their stock. The distribution of long barrows in some areas implies the presence of reasonably large numbers of people. The barrows may have marked significant points in the landscape, but their position suggests that it was the water frontage and valley slopes that were important as much as any pasture beyond. The rivers and streams appear to have formed the focal and economic hub much as they did for later farming communities. In the same way as the parish church, the monument may have provided evidence of ancestral rights to the holding and helped bind the community together. Here was evidence of feast, past ritual, ceremony as well as the selected bones of ancestors.

DRAINAGE PATTERNS AS TERRITORIES

Social organisation based on drainage patterns might in part help explain the role of causewayed enclosures, most of which in Wessex are on the watershed around the fringes of the landform. In terms of the drainage pattern, they occupy a frontier or liminal position in what might be considered a no man's land between one group of people and the next; a position ideally suited for inter-community gatherings, exchange, and games or perhaps ritualised warfare. The arrowheads at Crickley Hill (Dixon 1988) and Carn Brae (Mercer 1981) graphically illustrate the latter. Similar concentrations have been found on the slopes of Windmill Hill in Wiltshire (Brown et al. 2005), where the different types of leaf-shaped, petit-tranchet, barbed and tanged arrowheads indicate that related activities took place in the same location for over a millennium.

Crawford's recognition of common structural elements in the long barrows of the Severn drainage served to emphasise the importance of river systems in binding together groups of people in cultural and political units. Drainage patterns provide basic territorial catchment zones for hunters and agriculturists, both ancient and modern. Only in recent times has it been possible to modify this because of the possibilities of piping water into areas where it was formerly scarce. The massive artefact concentrations from the River Thames at London and of the Great Ouse, which are some of the largest in the country, imply that considerable populations lived alongside those stretches of the river and that proportionally fewer subsisted in the hinterland, as is the case today. The artefact distributions dramatically contrast with those of surviving monuments and that the latter might reflect what could have been atypical activity on the fringes of respective Neolithic polities is a sobering thought.

Where sufficient numbers of barrows have been located, for example, in the Wylye Valley of Wiltshire, a spacing of about 2km is frequent. The spacing suggests that they mark a series of land-units that focus on the river frontage (56). Similar frequencies occur in the middle reaches of the River Avon where, if anything, spacing is reduced to about 1km. It may even be that the pattern extends all the way to the coast, the Holdenhurst barrow being one of the final components in the chain. Similar spacing can be observed elsewhere. Along the River Kennet, the Beckhampton Road, Longstones, West and East Kennet, White Hill, Lockeridge long barrows, and, if Aubrey's description is correct, another at Manton or Clatford, indicates that spacings of about 2km might occur on the North Wiltshire Downs as well. A second tier can be observed some 2km to the south of them on Higher Downland incorporating Shepherds Shore, Rough Ridge Hill, Easton Down, Horton Down and Kitchen Barrow and at a little further distance Adam's Grave and West Woods Barrow. At 1.5km distant, some of these are a little close, but the larger gap between Adam's Grave and West Woods might indicate missing examples. Drewett (1975) suggested a series of potential territories on the South Downs with long barrows spaced about 4km apart and placed on the periphery of settled land units beyond the easily cultivated agricultural land. This might be modified in view of recent work, which proposed that the smaller mounds represented a subdivision of land-units already marked by the larger long barrows (Drewett 1986).

It is possible that this distribution represents a series of successively used sites as a group of people moved steadily along the valley, but with the human bones at West Kennet, for example, representing several generations, it seems more likely that each represents the holding of a separate family and that the landscape

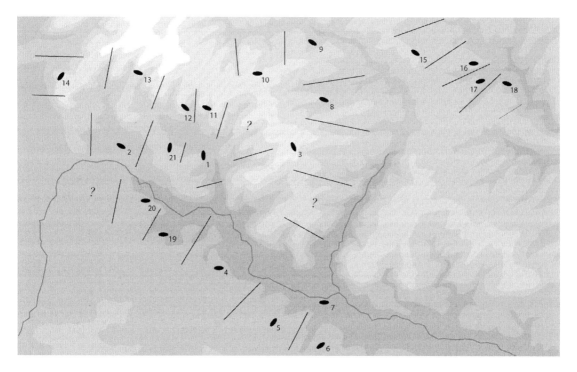

56 Long Barrows situated in the upper reaches of the Wylye Valley, with arbitrary land divisions drawn between them. 1. Heytesbury North Field; 2. King Barrow; 3. Knook; 4. Corton; 5. Boyton; 6. Stockton; 7. Sherrington; 8. Knook Down; 9. Imber; 10. Boles; 11. Norton Bavant; 12. Middleton; 13. Oxendean Down; 14. Arn Hill; 15. Kill Barrow; 16. Tilshead Lodge; 17. Old Ditch; 18. White Barrow; 19. St Leonards Church; 20. Dairy Plantation; 21. Scratchbury

was fully utilised. Assuming that many of these were in use contemporaneously, there is scarcely opportunity here for nomads or transhumants to pick their way through such utilised areas.

Certain examples lie at shorter intervals. South Street is just 500m from Longstones long barrow, but as they lay marginally either side of the ridge, it may be that they mark a common boundary between land units based in different valley zones, but elsewhere, it is more difficult to explain such 'pairings'. At Milston, two long barrows, one trapezoidal and the other short and rectangular, lay side by side not 100m apart on the valley floor. At Rockbourne in Hampshire, Knap Barrow and Gran's Barrow, are also less than 100m apart, as are two at Moody's Down, while two of three long mounds at Wonston (*57*) and Danebury lie within 200m of each other (*58*). On Cranborne Chase, the five long barrows (counting the 'tail' of the bank barrow) situated at the north-east end of the Dorset cursus in a space of less than a kilometre are all set along the same valley system, the closest less than 50m from each other.

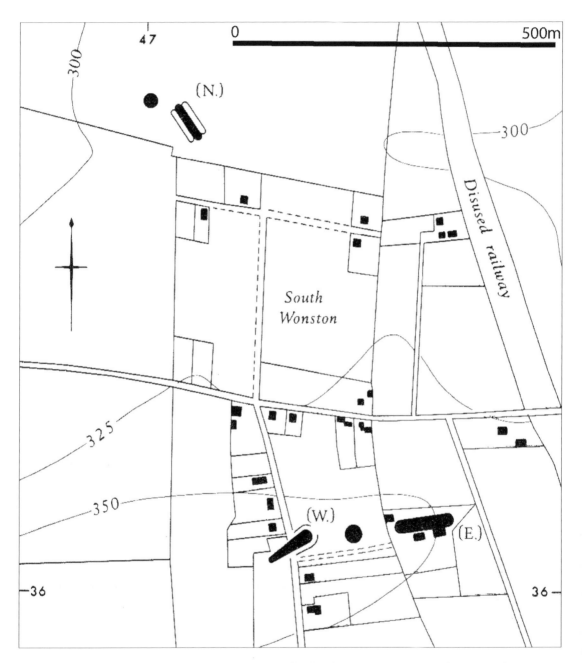

57 Three long barrows within close proximity of each other at Wonston, Hampshire. Note the position of the round barrows. *From RCHME 1979:© Crown copyright NMR*

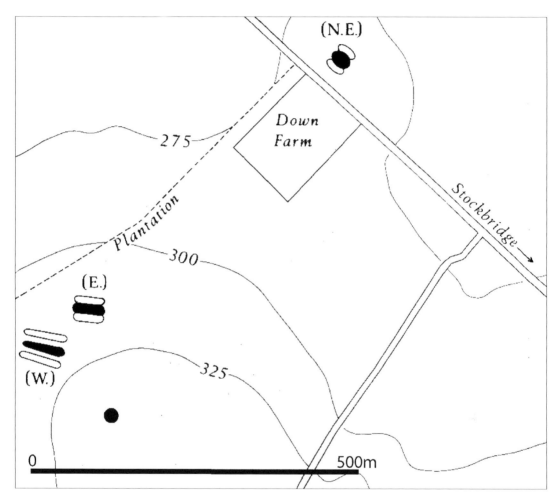

58 Three long barrows within close proximity to each other at Danebury, Hampshire. Note the single round barrow. *From RCHME 1979: © Crown copyright NMR*

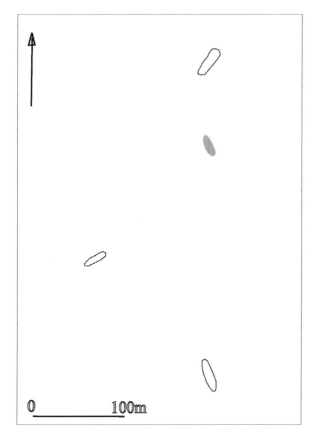

59 Plot of extant long barrow at Spellow Hills, Lincolnshire and three mortuary enclosures or levelled long barrows nearby. *Redrawn from Jones D. 1998 with permission*

In most cases the pairings or clusters are of different forms, thus at Danebury one is trapezoidal the other rectangular, at Milston one trapezoidal the other rectangular, and similarly at Moody's Down, Wonston and Alfriston. Only at Rockbourne are both trapezoidal and here they differ considerably in their proportions. However, aerial photography has introduced further complexity. An elongated mortuary enclosure was discovered just 200m to the north-west of Skendleby 1, making three large monuments within a short space. The two at Deadman's Graves, Claxby (*colour plate 25*), are joined by an ovoid enclosure, while the single mound at Spellow Hills is joined by three enclosures (*59*), two of them trapezoidal (Jones, D. 1998). There are other associations. Dilwyn Jones has drawn attention to the number of long mortuary enclosures with a single ring ditch close by, often at the broad end, highlighting 10 examples in Lincolnshire. There is currently no dating evidence to link them chronologically, but they recall the round mounds at the end of King Barrow and Pentridge (*colour plate 26*), Wonston West and Twinley in Hampshire, and it may be that there are many similar associations that remain unnoticed.

Increase in population coupled with intensification of intervention in the land may have resulted in subdivision of settled areas and construction of new mounds as Peter Drewett has suggested (Drewett 1986). The reason for the co-location of some barrows is more complex and it is difficult to account for some processes. Why, for example at Wayland's Smithy, Oxfordshire, a trapezoidal megalithic chambered barrow should be constructed over a smaller ovoid one (Atkinson 1965); or why West and East Kennet long barrows appear to have been enlarged but others in the vicinity not; or why the Milston pair, 39 and 40 (*26*), were constructed so close to each other. Extremely energetic social activity is implied by each of these constructions, each group responding in slightly different ways to economic and ceremonial imperatives, but there is an indication that focusing on individual 'sites' has obscured the complexity of relationships within a comparatively small tract of topography. There appears to be more to many long barrow sites than we had imagined.

7

LONG BARROWS, ANIMALS
AND PEOPLE

ANIMALS

Human relationships with animals will have changed significantly with increasing domestication. According to Tim Ingold (2000, 65-76), this is likely to be from a position of trust to one of domination, for while animals are perceived by hunters as carrying out a nurturing role and 'share' themselves with humans, the relationship is quite different to that of pastoralists, who control the life of the animal and therefore dominate it. Pastoralists certainly care for the animals and cannot subsist otherwise and they might be given as much, if not more, consideration than humans, for without adequate pasture, water and new blood, the herd will become diseased with potentially serious results for their human controllers. Nevertheless, compared to the relationship that hunters have with wild animals, they are essentially possessions or moveable wealth.

How viable herds of domestic animals were brought to these shores in the first place remains unclear. Small numbers can be transferred by boat, but it is difficult to envisage how sufficient numbers could be introduced at one attempt in order to allow a pastoralist lifestyle to be sustained from the outset. While there is no direct evidence, given the numbers of antlers used in the flint mines and the areas of grassland noted in the pre-barrow environments, there may have been deer lawns and some controlled herding or farming of red deer during the fifth millennium BC (see also Sharples 2000). Estimates of 100–400 antler picks were needed each year at Grimes Graves, up to some 150,000 for the site as a whole, needing a minimum of 120 deer in the vicinity (Clutton-Brock 1984). A process that ensured that the deer were well fed might also explain the unusually large antlers from the site. However, the overall picture is bound to be varied and perhaps regionalised.

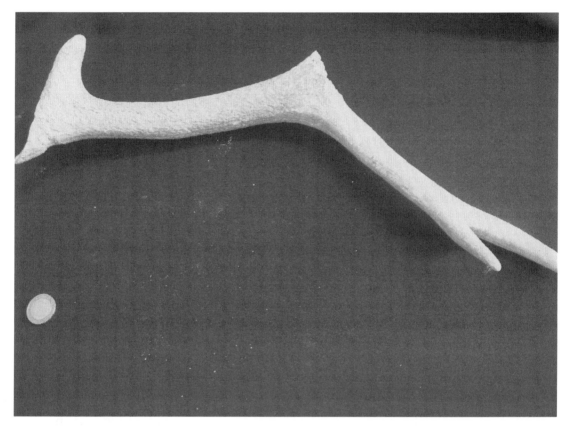

60 Antler from Woodford long barrow. *Courtesy of the Salisbury and South Wiltshire Museum*

Considerable numbers of red deer in the landscape might also be deduced from the antler picks often used in digging the side ditches at long barrows (*60*). In Wessex, six antlers were recovered from the mound and another from the primary ditch fill at South Street, while at least ten antler picks, two rakes, and eighteen fragments were discarded during construction of the mound at Beckhampton Road. Five of those found on the buried surface were arranged in two neat piles. In one, a pick was neatly and precisely aligned on top of another, while in the other a rake was carefully placed on top of two picks. The arrangements recall the piles of antler tools found in flint mines, where ethnographic evidence has suggested that it may have been part of a ritual process to leave tools behind (Topping 1997). While at least three antlers from Fussell's Lodge had been shed and collected, red deer bones from primary positions at this and other sites infer that venison was being eaten. At Skendleby two red deer bones were found in the façade trench and on the old ground surface, at Nutbane on the old ground surface and in the mortuary enclosure.

The presence of animal remains in long barrow deposits was encountered at an early stage of investigation. In his excavation of King Barrow in 1801, William Cunnington was astonished at the amount of animal bone encountered within the matrix of the mound: 'pieces of Stags Horns, animal and human bones, boars tusks' and the 'entire skeleton of a horse'. Almost 'the whole of the floor' beneath the mound was found to be 'covered with animal bones of almost every description … (all amongst) charred wood some of which adhered to the bones half cremated by fire … '. Cunnington was evidently concerned and wondered how it could be explained.

He consulted his butcher and between them they were able to recognise cattle, pig and horse and the butcher realised that certain bones of the animals were unusual. When Cunnington took the skull and horns of a large bovid, presumably aurochs, from Knook Barrow to him, he declared it to be 'larger than any he ever saw of the ox kind'. Regarding bones from Sherrington Barrow, the butcher declared that the teeth were not of any animal that he was familiar with and in the case of an animal from Knook Barrow wondered whether 'some of the gentlemen belonging to the Board of Agriculture might tell what kind of ox it was' (Field 2006).

At the east end of the long mound in Heytesbury North Field were the 'Heads and Horns of a great many oxen, stags horns etc'. Similarly, at the east end of Boles Barrow, he found the 'Heads and Horns of seven or more oxen' although it is not clear whether these were found together with the human bones or in a separate deposit. Further excavations into the mound by (the later) William Cunnington revealed the horn cores of four more oxen bringing the total represented to eleven. The latter group were found 'about three yards within the barrow, towards the southeast and about a foot above the base … . They occurred in a space a little more than a yard square. They were in no regular position and were accompanied by a few metatarsals'. The specific mention of the metatarsals is particularly interesting as the presence of the feet of cattle have been recorded from other long barrows as well.

Thurnam encountered similar bones, frequently the skulls and feet of cattle. At either end of the base of the mound at Tilshead Lodge he found a domestic cattle skull. Close to that at the east end he found the feet bones in situ along with several deer antlers. The second skull had six or seven cervical vertebrae attached, the atlas and dentata each broken in two 'cleanly cleft as if by great violence'. In the Stonehenge cursus long barrow, Amesbury 42, he found part of a skull along with the foot bones of four or five cattle all with the phalangal bones in place and occasionally the ankles. Thurnam reasoned that the cattle were killed as part of a funeral rite and that these pieces represented the parts of the animals not used in a feast. The entire portions of the feet, as well as head

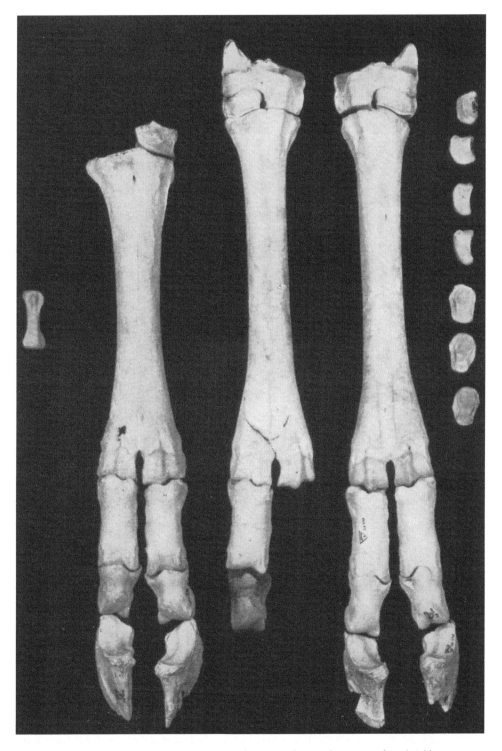

61 Cattle feet bones from Fussell's Lodge long barrow. *Photograph courtesy of Paul Ashbee*

and neck, indicated that these parts had been held together with flesh at the time of deposition (Thurnam 1869, 182). However, in Amesbury 14, south-west of Stonehenge and in Norton Bavant long barrow, there were broken leg bones, fleshy parts that might be used for feasting.

Bones of aurochs, wild bison-like cattle, were recovered from the forecourt trenches and the mortuary enclosure at Nutbane and there were other fragments from the primary silts of the ditch. Based on its large size, the skull found on top of the cairn by Cunnington at Knook Barrow also appears to have been an aurochs. Most cattle deposits, however, appear to have been domestic species. Although not well preserved, cattle bones were found in primary positions on the old ground surface and in the façade trench at Skendleby 2, while fragments of domestic cattle along with a human fibula were also present amongst occupation debris at the east end of Willerby Wold. At South Street, there were ten mandible fragments in the buried soil as well as leg bones and feet, while four articulated vertebrae were found in the primary ditch fill.

Most of the animal bone from the earliest contexts at Fussell's Lodge was also of domestic cattle (*61*). A cattle skull was found at the end of the mortuary deposit where it had been treated in a similar manner to the human bone. A small heap of foot bones representing three feet, some of them articulated, was recovered from the surface of the flint cairn and others from within it. Further remains of a vertebral column from a domestic ox, with ribs, mandible and other bones, but minus the head and legs, were found lying on the primary silts of the ditch (Ashbee 1966). This appears to have been deposited when held together by tendons and subsequently disturbed.

Repeatedly, it is the head and feet that are found, while the rest of the body, the fleshy parts that are good to eat, are generally absent. If feasting was involved and in view of the number of skulls at some sites it is hard not to think in those terms, then it must have taken place off-site. The position of the pieces is also intriguing, frequently located at the east end close to, but separate from, the human bone deposits. At Beckhampton Road the remains of three skulls were situated along the axial fence, one placed at either end, with a third between them in a similar arrangement to that at Tilshead Lodge, while in two cases, at Knook and Fussell's Lodge, skulls were placed on the summit of the cairn. This was presumably much more than decoration for there were undoubtedly clan or kinship signals and supernatural implications. The animal may have been supernatural protector of the mound or the hunched and parabolic profiled flint cairn itself may have been representative of the animal. Certainly the horn-shaped forecourts of some long barrows point to a certain symbolic representation and pre-occupation with cattle, perhaps a belief system involving animism. In such systems, the interdependence of humans and animals, both in the material and supernatural worlds plays a central role (Ingold 2000, 111-31). Some mounds might even be perceived as being constructed in a manner that emulates the skeleton, with the fencing representing an axial backbone and series of ribs. Where skulls are present, they are not casually discarded but appear to be deliberately positioned. Those at the east end of mounds are invariably placed adjacent to but in front of human bones. The heads might imply that the spirits are present to protect and sustain the human, but equally facilitate interchange and metamorphosis of human and animal spirits. The feet might indicate that animals were no longer free spirits or alternatively have helped to facilitate metaphysical movement. The whole process of slaughtering and feasting on animals made certain that the supernatural process continued and ensured rebirth and regeneration.

Stuart Piggott (1962b) drew attention to 'head and hoofs' burials, a phenomenon widespread in time and space across northern Europe. The process involved killing the animal and feasting on the flesh while the skin and bones form the sacrifice. The hide with the head and feet intact is hung on a pole or frame or folded up and placed in a tomb. It may be that similar processes took place in the UK during the Neolithic. Perhaps just as likely, the hide with head attached was worn in some ceremony, from which the wearer might obtain the persona and attributes of the animal and assist in the transformation process during rites of renewal.

Pigs are less well represented at most sites, but there are nevertheless a few remains found in early contexts. On the old ground surface and in the façade trench at Skendleby 2, and in the mortuary enclosure and forecourt trenches at Nutbane were a few bones; while bones of a single pig were present in the buried soil at South Street, where its small stature led to the conclusion that it was domestic. Nearby, at Horslip, bones representing at least 13 pigs were found in primary contexts. In all these cases, occasional or isolated bones, presumably the remnants of meals appear to have become incorporated on old ground surfaces and into features rather than being deliberately positioned. Hanging Grimston, in Yorkshire, is rather different, for here there were 20 pig mandibles arranged in 4 piles around the facade (Kinnes 1992). Pig had apparently assumed the importance afforded to cattle in the southern long barrows. It may be that the local environment suited pig herding as has been suggested at Runnymede, a Neolithic settlement adjacent to the River Thames (Serjeantson 2006), or it may represent a precursor of Grooved Ware traditions in which pig became important as a feasting animal. It also recalls a pile of 12–15 sheep mandibles found at the base of a flint-mine shaft at Blackpatch in Sussex. These were encircled by burnt stones and well-knapped flint implements and appear to be a structured deposit. Pete Topping (2005, 74) has suggested that they are similar to many of the 'magic piles' or 'idols', offerings or petitions to the spirit world, recorded by Catlin and other explorers among the nineteenth-century plains tribes in North America.

Traces of sheep and/or goat, which are almost indistinguishable as skeletal material are present in some long mounds, but in very much smaller quantities. Their small bones are easier to decay and may be under-represented in the record (Legge 1991). At South Street, skull fragments, ribs and leg bones were found in the buried soil and a sheep or goat humerus was present just above the primary silt of the ditch at Fussell's Lodge, while at Horslip some 15 individuals were represented by isolated bones found in a primary context. Like the remnants of pig bones all, however, appear to have accumulated as domestic debris.

A single dog bone was recovered at Horslip, where it appears to have been treated no differently from the other bones. Its incorporation alongside other isolated bones suggests that it might be food debris and, taboos aside, there is no reason why dog could not have been eaten, particularly if it were a young example (cf. for example attitudes of the Plains Indians pers. comm. Pete Topping). A fox skull was found in the filling of a posthole on the forecourt at Nutbane. At the time it was considered that as a burrowing animal it may be a modern example, but this might seem overcautious given that the rest of the skeleton was not present and it might instead have signalled clan, spirit or kinship identities.

Isolated horse bones occur at some sites, a tooth at Fussell's Lodge, a single bone from the primary ditch silt at Horslip, while a tooth was found in a chamber at the Nympsfield chambered tomb (Saville 1979). At King Barrow, a complete horse skeleton was said to be present. None of this evidence is from absolutely secure contexts, however, and it is generally thought that the first introduction of horse came during the Bronze Age. The evidence here is cumulative, but cannot be used to take the matter further. The tooth from Fussell's Lodge was in the upper level of the flint cairn and may have moved down the stratigraphy from above and the same might have been the case for the single bone at Horslip. At Nympsfield the bone was found amongst material backfilling the forecourt and chamber area following a modern excavation, while at King Barrow, the position of the skeleton towards the edge of the mound could mean that it was a later insertion. For the moment it is better to be overcautious, but the number of examples is accruing, for example at Runnymede (Serjeantson 2006), and there is also evidence of horse from later Neolithic sites, Durrington Walls and Grimes Graves to take into account (Albarella 2006). It may be that eventually the introduction of horse will need to be reconsidered.

Birds are frequently reported as present, particularly large ones with striking plumage. Cunnington commented on the presence of bird bones on the floors and pavements amongst the charred wood and ashes at King Barrow, where they were found among an array of other animal bones. Again at Old Ditch, there was an abundance of larger bird bones and a 'shovel full of small bird bones deposited together'. At Knook Barrow, along with human bones, bird bones were found on the pavement, 'some of which appeared like the bones of a Heron'. On the floor of the Sherrington barrow, were the bones of 'a large bird', while at Amesbury 14, south-west of Stonehenge, Thurnam found the 'entire skeleton of a goose' and, attempting to explain it, referred to the testimony of Caesar that although the British bred geese for pleasure and amusement, they considered it a taboo to eat them (Thurnam 1869, 183).

Heron has a widespread distribution which might parallel the Neolithic situation (Wingfield Gibbons *et al.* 1993, 48-9) particularly given milder weather and less persecution. The tree-lined valleys of the chalk streams provide good nesting sites and they can be found today along the Avon, Nadder, Wylye and other rivers. There is a possibility that the heron was misidentified, however, given the known presence of crane in the Neolithic (pers. comm. Dale Serjeantson). Crane is skeletally similar but slightly larger than heron and its white plumage might have proved attractive to local people. On Orkney, sea-eagles have been found in Neolithic tombs and Andy Jones (1998) has argued that animals found in such places might be totemic emblems reflecting how the location was perceived within the landscape. White-tailed sea-eagle was also found in the south ditch of the Coneybury henge, near Stonehenge (Maltby, in Richards 1990, 150-4) and, while it could have moved inland to scavenge, it is nevertheless some way out of its usual habitat. The skull of a phalarope, a wading bird, was found at the end of a flint-mine gallery at Grimes Graves in Norfolk, at least 100km from the contemporary coastline. Along with a ground axe from Cornwall, it formed part of a deliberately placed arrangement being flanked by two antler picks with their tines pointing inwards. Given the landscape context, each of these birds is unusual; according to Jones (1998) sea-eagles are difficult to catch while herons nest in the canopy of tall trees. However, such difficulties only enhance quest-like challenges. Native Americans catch eagles by digging a pit to sit in, covering it with vegetation and holding a small bird as bait above it. As the eagle pounces they grab its talons (pers. comm. Pete Topping). Like the stone axe brought from a distance, such birds might have special value, perhaps as totemic references, but they could also be perceived as having supernatural powers or represent sky deities. Unlike humans they can fly and they can observe the land in a way that humans cannot.

HUMAN BONES

The range of situations in which human bone was incorporated in deposits makes it difficult to determine whether burial was an incidental or primary factor in the function of barrows. While mounds such as Thickthorn Down, Therfield

Heath, Royston, South Street and Beckhampton Road contained no burials, others held only small numbers: Alfriston one, Abingdon two, neither of which can be said to represent a communal tomb; if burial was the primary purpose then the major part of the community must have been interred elsewhere. It has been suggested that bodies were excarnated, laid out on platforms or scaffolds perhaps at causewayed enclosures, for the flesh to rot, from where the bones were collected and placed in tombs. Indeed recent dating programmes of material from Windmill Hill and the nearby West Kennet long barrow indicate that this is a real possibility (Whittle *et al* 2011). Large numbers could equally have been deposited in other places, such as caves, trees, or rivers. In contrast, however, some long barrows contain bones representing greater numbers of bodies. At Boles Barrow at least 17 were mentioned, at Heytesbury North Field 10-20 and at Fussell's Lodge 53-57. More recent analysis of bones from the latter site, however, suggests that the initial figure provided was an overestimate and the number was closer to 34 (Wysocki *et al* 2007).

A single contracted skeleton was found lying on its right side at Winterbourne Stoke Crossroads, a long barrow of considerable length and height, while the bones of a single individual were also found at Figheldean 31, a barrow of much lesser stature. The ligaments of the latter, Thurnam thought, had decayed and the bones became disarticulated before burial. He commented that the bones were not always in their correct position and implied that the skeleton had been reassembled (Thurnam 1869, 184). It was the human bones that really interested Thurnam. He was disappointed that Cunnington's skulls were not available for study but by 1869 his own excavations had recovered 27 skulls from primary contexts in 10 different long barrows. Having measured the ratio of length to breadth, or the cephalic index, he considered that they were unusually long: indeed so long and narrow that he could find no parallels in nineteenth-century Europe (Thurnam 1869 198-9).

At Alfriston, a pit was discovered central to the long axis of the mound, which contained a single-crouched skeleton. It lay with its head to the north and facing east. In a possibly oval grave pit in a similar position at Abingdon, two crouched burials were placed with heads at the opposite sides of the pit. One was a woman with a ground-flint knife placed near her head, while the other, a male, was accompanied by a jet belt slider that lay at his hip. A leaf-shaped arrowhead found in a disturbed context nearby may also have come from the burial. The burial at Alfriston is probably female and until the time of death she was in good health, while at Abingdon both the man and woman were of a similar age, 30-35, and could have been partners. Why they should be singled out for this treatment is not clear. It may be that they were of high status, leaders, shamen, or were revered for some particularly outstanding feat or action. Or it could be that they were captives or sacrificial victims or had

62 Primary burials at Wor Barrow. Six burials were recorded. Those numbered one, two and six lay side by side, the skull of two missing and that of six decayed, the bones of the others had been placed in a pile in the north-east corner of the arrangement. *Pitt Rivers 1898*

contracted some disease.

At Old Ditch, there were three evidently complete skeletons, two placed side by side with their heads to the north and the third lying transversely. The latter was the largest, though the bones were in poor preservation. Just a metre off centre at the base of the Knook Down long barrow was a complete skeleton, with head to the north-east (the barrow is oriented to the east) but no accompanying artefacts. Cunnington commented that it must have been an elderly man, for the skull was 'very thick, the teeth were all gone, one of the arms had been fractured and had been 'set' though badly'. Just over a metre to the east of this were three more skeletons similarly oriented, although there were no further comments regarding detail.

Four skeletons lay on the pavement at Skendleby 1 in a crouched position and there were odd bones from four further individuals. They were crowded close together and overlay each other, but were precisely placed within the confines of the pavement, which implies that there may have been some kind of constraining structure or fence in position at the time that they were deposited. In addition, remains of further bodies in an eroded and weathered condition were present and thought to represent parts of individuals re-interred from elsewhere and not contemporary with the others. Six skeletons were present at Wor Barrow (*62* and *63*). They were laid within a similarly small area, just 2.4 x 1m. Three were crouched with their heads to the south and the other three represented by assembled bones placed in a group to one side with the long bones parallel.

Like a number of sites at Heytesbury North Field, the human bones, some in poor condition, lay 'crossing each other in every direction' and were reported as being in a complete state of disarray in a very similar manner to those at

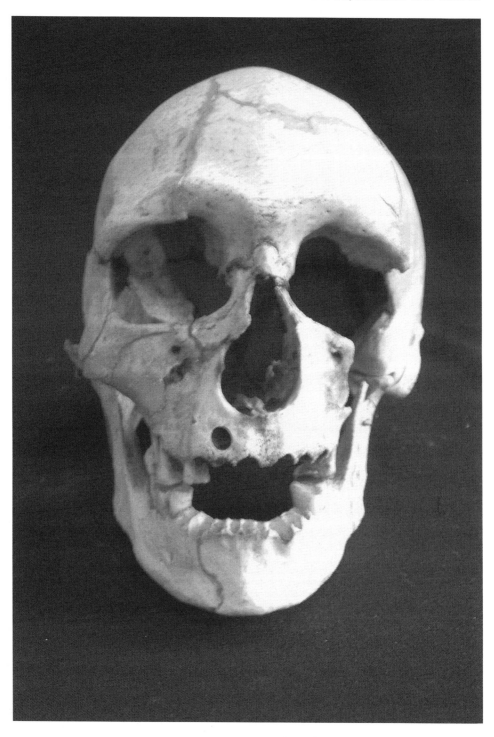

63 Skull of skeleton no 5, one of the primary burials at Wor Barrow. *Courtesy of the Salisbury and South Wiltshire Museum*

Boles Barrow just 2.5km to the north. As a farmer from Imber had offered the assistance of four of his workers, Cunnington set out to excavate the latter mound in the late summer of 1801. At 3.2m deep, beneath a mound of stones was a pavement of 'regularly laid' flint nodules on which were the remains of 'a great many human bodies, but like those at Heytesbury North Field, placed in no regular order, as upon a skull we found the backbones and ribs of another skeleton, and upon the neck of another, two thighbones'. The trench may have been cambered or stepped for safety, for Cunnington mentions that at the base they only had time to uncover a small area of about 3 x 2m, yet there were the skulls of 13 individuals. Many of the bones were in good condition and the teeth quite white. One piece of skull appeared to have been sliced off so neatly that Cunnington thought that it must have been cut off with a sword, but it was probably a trepanation, where a roundel of bone had been cut out of the skull with a flint knife in order to relieve pressure either actual or metaphysical. Only one small fragment of bone was burnt, although in contrast to King Barrow, there was no other evidence of fire and it must be presumed that any funeral pyre was elsewhere.

When Thurnam reopened the mound in 1864 and found the bones left by Cunnington, he recovered fragments of the skull of a girl of eight or ten years old along with the jaw of a second child. Many of the skull fragments were thought to have been cleft or smashed as a result of some violent procedure. Reinvestigated by the later William and Henry Cunnington in 1885 and 1886, three further skulls and many other human bones were found. Scattered around the edge of a 'ritual' pit were other human bones of a different colour to those found on the pavement and which were presumed to have represented a skeleton that once lay on top of the pit, but which had been disturbed by William Cunnington's activities in 1801. Its cranium had been crushed by a large sarsen boulder but the contrast in colour and the circumstances and position suggested that they may have represented an earlier interment. The excavators concurred with Thurnam regarding the damage to the skulls and indicated that in their view there was no doubt that most were killed by wounds to the left side of the head or to the area of the eye. They noted that a neck vertebra had been cut in two by a sharp implement and concluded that the individual must have been beheaded. Some skulls were found placed upright and the fact that in one case a vertebra had lodged itself over the left condyle of a lower mandible implied that at least some of these bones had been deposited in an unfleshed state. Many of the bones had been gnawed by rodents and the long bones were evidently found in a less than perfect condition, implying that they had been exposed to the weather at some stage. Among them, two pieces of leg bone had evidently been sharpened to a point.

In some instances burial deposits were contained within extremely small areas.

64 Group of human bone from within the mortuary area at Fussell's Lodge. *Photograph courtesy of Paul Ashbee*

The bones in the Norton Bavant mound were found to comprise remains of at least 18 individuals all confined to an area of no more than 2.4 x 1 x 0.5m high. They simply would not all fit in if they were in a fleshed state. Limb bones were often absent and the amount of mixing of bones led Thurnam to the conclusion that these must have been collected and placed there from earlier burials. It was a similar case at Tilshead East long barrow, where the remains of eight individuals were found compacted, this time 'cemented together', into a comparably small area 1.2m long and less than 0.5m deep. Thurnam's excavations at Tilshead Lodge uncovered just two contracted skeletons lying closely adjacent to each other, but they had been doubled up so tightly that although all of the bones were found in situ, he considered that 'very unusual means had been resorted to … or the flesh (but not the ligaments holding the body together) had been suffered to decay before burial'.

At Fussell's Lodge, bones were deposited in five piles within a restricted area at the east end of the mortuary enclosure (*64*). Fragments of others were found in an underlying pit as well as in the overlying flint cairn. While all parts of the skeleton were present, there were fewer ribs and shoulder blades and, in particular, a lack of smaller bones, fingers, toes and knee bones. The explanation supporting Thurnam's observation was that the bones had been moved from a prior location, some perhaps when the bodies were only partly defleshed, or perhaps that the smaller bones had fallen through a scaffold. The condition of the bones indicated that some had received greater weathering than others; some had been gnawed by rodents and far from representing a single burial event, were thought to represent an accumulation of body parts over several generations. Whether they were deposited within the mortuary enclosure during a single or several episodes is equally unclear, but the stacks of skulls and long bones seems to imply some special event, with earlier deposits scattered in the process. The nature of the occasion is unclear, but it would appear to have been connected to the construction of an overlying cairn since the piles of bones had been preserved from disturbance by animals. Some of the bones had been crushed by the weight of the flint nodules of the cairn which lay immediately over and alongside. It seems possible that the bones, both ancient and contemporary, were deposited as part of a commemoration process. If so, they may have represented the stacked up genealogies of the local community and proof of inherited occupancy. The building of a cairn covered the evidence, prohibited continued use and drew a line over the way in which the site was used.

Following Cunnington's excavation at the eastern end of Old Ditch long barrow, in which he found no burials, Thurnam reinvestigated the site 'at its very broadest and highest part'. At a depth of more than 3m and beneath a layer of black earth, he found a small cairn of large flints, beneath which, and on a pavement of similar flints, was a pile of burnt human bones thought to represent one individual. The cairn and pavement displayed evidence of heat, many of the flints being very brittle and of a red or blue colour. The condition of the flint suggests that the bones were burnt in situ. Cunnington had previously noted the presence of a large quantity of 'burnt bones' in Knook Barrow and this subsequently prompted Thurnam to reinvestigate the matter. He dug at the north-east end and found more burnt bones together with burnt flints. Here, however, despite extensively investigating the base of the mound, no evidence for a complete skeleton was encountered. Thurnam returned to Bratton long barrow; another mound formerly investigated by Cunnington and at a depth of 2.5m encountered a deposit of charred bones thought to be representative of, at most, two adults. Again no complete skeleton could be found and it was as though parts of bodies in a semi-fleshed state, or parts of skeletons had been carried from elsewhere to be burnt.

One of Thurnam's chief observations when considering the skulls was that many appeared to have been split or fractured by a blunt instrument and he compared them closely with anthropological examples, in particular, one from Bolivia where similar features had been made by a stone implement. Detailed examination convinced him that these injuries were incurred during life and certainly before burial. Familiar with contemporary and historic burial practices across the world, and from 'repeated and minute examinations of the bones' he was content that the long barrows were not simply ossuaries or bone houses, but concluded that the burials represented sacrificial victims (Thurnam 1869, 185) and concurred with his contemporary William Greenwell (1865) who had excavated long barrows in Yorkshire, that cannibalism may have been involved. Such features have less often been found in modern excavations and Thurnam's description of fractured skulls has been largely discounted and explained by natural fracture due to the weight of the mound. However, more recently Rick Shulting has investigated some 350 skulls from Neolithic sites, among them examples from 20 long barrows, and was able to distinguish between original breaks in the skull and those broken after death either as a result of disturbance of the burial deposit or the crushing effects of collapsed mound components. Amongst them, 26 examples of healed and unhealed wounds were identified, of which some fractures were evidently fatal. In nine cases, it was considered that the wound may have been the cause of death. A blunt instrument had been used, possibly an antler tine and in one case perhaps a ground axe. One came from Norton Bavant and there were three examples from Fussell's Lodge with healed head wounds, one a possible trepanation. Schulting presumed that conflict in the Neolithic was small-scale and largely restricted to feuds, cattle raids and violence related to revenge (Schulting 2002: Schulting and Wysocki 2005).

Despite the suggestions of violence at Boles Barrow, the skeletal material also included three children and an infant, but there are other sites, for example, at Fussell's Lodge and Skendleby 1, where it may be possible to obtain a greater glimpse of the local community. At Fussell's Lodge, about 30 were adults almost equally divided into male and female and the rest children of various ages. Of the eight skeletons at Skendleby, only one was definitely male and a second possibly so. Three and possibly a fourth were young adult females, while one was a child aged no more than six. The male exhibited 'extreme muscularity' and there was no evidence of disease or injury or rheumatism, indeed all bodies appeared to be relatively healthy. In three cases there was evidence that they had favoured a squatting posture. Where present teeth were healthy and in good order in contrast to those at Boles Barrow where the teeth were considerably worn, even on a child of about 12, and often at an oblique angle of 45° or more. In one jaw, the enamel had been completely worn away on the grinding surfaces of the teeth. At Old Ditch, while the teeth were considered very sound, they had evidently been ground flat as though they had been filed down. Cunnington recorded that this was commonplace among the skeletons found in long barrows. The likeliest cause is that diet contained grit from the grinding of foodstuff, but there may be other reasons, for example, where teeth were used as a vice to grip material in a repeated manner. Analysis of oxygen isotopes from bones found at Fussell's Lodge and Bolesbarrow indicated more of a mixed diet than those towards the Cotswolds (the reader is referred to Smith and Brickley's (2009) more recent study that considers the evidence for diet and disease in greater detail).

While large numbers of individuals are present at some sites the bones have evidently been subject to different processes and retention perhaps over a considerable period. While some mounds contain no burial at all, in some instances several burials seem to have occurred just prior to the covering of the site and may have provided the catalyst for that action. Although there was a greater degree of completeness among the human bones, particularly among the latest of the deposits, in other respects animal and human bones appear to have received similar treatment.

CULTURAL ARTEFACTS

The scarcity of cultural artefacts was found worthy of comment by Thurnam. A single elongated, almost phallic-shaped nodule, some 20cm in length, with blades struck from one end was found close to the arm of a skeleton in the Winterbourne Stoke Crossroads barrow (56 and *colour plate 27*). Amongst the remnants of over 18 skeletons at Norton Bavant was a flint hammerstone, while from Giant's Grave, Fyfield Hill a leaf-shaped arrowhead was recovered from adjacent to a skull. Having found similar artefacts in Adam's Grave and Rodmarton chambered barrows, Thurnam considered these to be 'the long barrow type of arrowhead' (Thurnam 1869, 194). Four lozenge-shaped arrowheads were found in Pistle Down long barrow, Verwood, Dorset, when excavated in 1828 by Dr Wake-Smart (Warne 1866, 16) but little else is known about any associated deposits, while two flint arrowheads were found in primary silt at Badshot Lea, one leaf the other half broken, but evidently

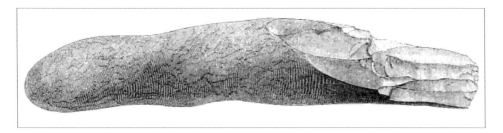

65 Flint implement found accompanying a crouched skeleton with its knees closely drawn up during excavations at the east end of Winterbourne Stoke Crossroads long barrow (*Thurnam 1869*). Phallic shaped flint nodules and chalk carvings have frequently been found in flint mines (for example, at Grimes Graves), one was also found in the primary silt of the ditch at Thickthorn Down long barrow. *Drew and Piggott 1936*

lozenge-shaped and both were found in association with cattle and red deer bones. A ground-flint knife was associated with one of the skeletons at Abingdon and a leaf-shaped arrowhead was found not far away, though the precise context was obscured as a result of early medieval disturbance. A flint scraper was found in both postholes at the site.

Ground axes are all but missing from primary contexts. This is quite surprising given their ubiquity within the Neolithic as a whole. The one example is itself unusual. It is a thin-butted (wide in plan) flint axe of rectangular cross-section from Jullieberrie's Grave, which was recovered from the turf core at the heart of the mound. Such axes are found as an early component of the Neolithic across northern Europe, but are rare in the UK. When they are recorded it is usually as chance finds and it is invariably suggested that they are ethnographic strays that have been discarded by collectors. But there are others that are difficult to account for extending from Canterbury along the Thames to west Surrey and northwards as far as Yorkshire, some of them of Group XX rock (Field 1984, 90-3). It may be relevant that the chambered long barrows in the Medway gap at Addington and Coldrum have been thought to display north European characteristics (Piggott 1935) and the implication is that Scandinavian or north-European influence may have been reaching Kent at this time.

There appears to have been an episode of almost impromptu knapping at some sites. At South Street almost 300 flakes were found beneath the mound in the buried soil, 20 core rejuvenation flakes and 11 cores as well as a fire damaged bifacially retouched piece thought to be a sickle. In addition there was a broken flake of Portland Chert that may have been brought from the south coast although was not outside its normal distribution. This material need not relate to the mound at all, but it would have been recognised as human, perhaps ancestral, debris and announced details concerning past use of the site. Nine-

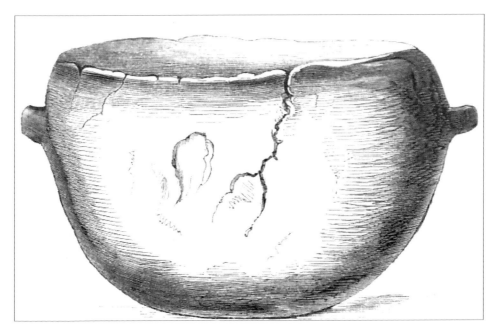

66 Neolithic lugged bowl from the excavation of Norton Bavant long barrow. *Thurnam 1869*

hundred struck flakes were found in primary positions at Alfriston, although just ten had been utilised. The reason for this is obscure. The resultant tools were not discovered and must have been discarded elsewhere. In contrast, of only 27 struck pieces found in primary positions at Horslip, 5 were fragmentary cores and at Kilham there were similarly low numbers, just 11 flakes and a scraper were found in the mortuary enclosure.

The blade end of a chisel made from the long bone of an undisclosed animal was recovered from the midden material overlying the 'wall' of stones at Skendleby 1. Phillips the excavator pointed to the similarities with a chisel found in a chambered long barrow at Temple Bottom in Wiltshire (Anon 1866). The only item of personal adornment came from Abingon, where a jet or shale belt slider was found with one skeleton. These are unusual in the south, but more frequent in Yorkshire, where deposits of jet are available along the cliffs and where an example from Whitegrounds is dated to 3500–2900 cal. BC (HAR 5587).

Little pottery has been recovered, either from burial contexts or the mounds as a whole. While sherds from seven pots were recovered at Fussell's Lodge, only two were complete, a carinated bowl with lugs on the shoulder (*colour plate 28*) along with a small plain bowl, both of which came from the burial area. The rest were deposited as sherds, having been broken elsewhere. There was a second, fragmentary carinated piece, decorated above and below the carination with pin-prick like stabs. The others were simple open bowls, most of them decorated on the rim or body with vertical strokes. Thurnam (1869, 195) recorded the presence of a complete lugged bowl amongst the human bone at Norton Bavant (66) and a bowl was also found with the burial deposit at Kilham (Greenwell 1877). Only at Haddenham were complete pots of Mildenhall Ware found in the forecourt. (Hodder and Shand 1988, 352).

Elsewhere pottery was fragmentary or simply collections of sherds. Almost all excavated sites produced several pieces. At Skendleby 2, for example, ten sherds were found in a primary context; at Willerby Wold, three were found in the primary silt of the ditch and there was also sherds from several vessels, none of them complete, from among the occupation debris at the eastern end of the mound. Fragments from the same vessel were found some distance apart. Three sherds were recovered at South Street, two from a carinated bowl, while at Kilham, Grimston Ware sherds were recovered from the old land surface, burial area and primary ditch silt. Much pottery was also recovered from the old ground surface at Skendleby 1 and from the various midden deposits at the site, but most of it was in small-comminuted fragments.

In general, deposits of cultural material are meagre. Where it does occur, it often appears to be deposited as odd sherds and occasional broken bowls which, like much of the human bone, appears to have been brought from elsewhere. It may also have had a similar role to play in the regeneration process as the animal and human bones, as the pots themselves have undergone a transformative process during firing (Darvill 2004, 196). Only at Abingdon are the artefacts associated with burials rather different, marking the emergence of an increasing importance of the individual.

8

PERCEPTION, TRADITION AND CHANGE: THE METAMORPHOSIS OF MONUMENTS

FUNCTION

The massive and monumental long mound constructed alongside the River Nene at Raunds, Northamptonshire (Windell *et al.* 1990, 9: Healy and Harding 2003, 4), comprised the turf taken from an area the size of a football pitch. Like other mounds of the period constructed completely or in part of turf at Holdenhurst, Hampshire (Piggott 1937a), Beckhampton, South Street, Avebury (Ashbee *et al.* 1979), or Therfield Heath (Phillips 1935), it is generally considered to be a monument for ritual, burial and ceremonial purposes, but the low-lying location at Raunds coupled with the construction material would hardly make it stand out from its surroundings. Camouflaged by vegetation and soil, it would instead mimic the natural land within the immediate environs until a thin capping of gravel placed over it provided a contrast. How this cutting of turf, a significant alteration to the natural environment affecting animals and insects alike, was conducted or perceived is unclear, but such damage to the land surface is injurious and without good reason and appropriate offerings, metaphysical constituents might be displeased (e.g. Humphrey 1995). There was much more to this than just building something. The same might be true of more durable constructions; the Devil's Den, a free-standing sarsen chamber constructed in Clatford Bottom, near Marlborough, Wiltshire, once thought to have been covered with an earthen mound and now isolated within a ploughed field, formerly lay all but camouflaged amongst a natural accumulation of sarsen boulders said to be so numerous that it was possible to walk along the valley floor stepping from one to another without putting foot on the ground (Brentnall 1946, 420-1). Such unusual accumulations of stone might be perceived with more than awe and astonishment and it is easy to imagine how such places might attract legend, tradition and belief, perhaps of ancestors, much as they did in the folklore of historic times. Movement of any one earthfast boulder might be carried out only with due ceremony and appropriate caution in order to avoid disturbance and displeasure of supernatural elements, but on doing so, like the removal of turf to create the mound at Raunds, a natural sequence of events with immediate environmental impact would be quickly set in motion. Depending on how much soil went with the turf, this would involve seed germination and colonisation of plants, vigorous growth and result in the presence of a completely new flora or a barren zone devoid of life.

There are other implications. In historic times, the chalkland valleys containing the unusual streams of sarsen boulders have been considered awe inspiring and worthy of comment by travel writers such as Daniel Defoe, antiquarians such as Aubrey, historians such as Hoare, and geologists such as M.J. Osborn White. Traditions and myths have become attached to stones and, at the Rollright Stones, in Oxfordshire, folklore considered them to be solidified individuals (Grinsell 1976). At the beginning of the Neolithic, roughly 6000 years ago, perception of such places will have been very different from our modern understanding. Such places may have been considered sacred or even taboo locations dwelt in by ancestors.

Given the folklore, and ethnographic parallels (for example Parker Pearson and Ramilisonina 1998), it is easy to imagine how stone may take on certain (special) meanings as perhaps ancestral beings, but less obvious that in places devoid of that material other objects such as trees might take on similar roles. Why turf should be considered of special interest is not clear, although as the primary feed of stock it would be of considerable importance in a regeneration or renewal process. It is certainly possible to build with it – and to burn it. But it is also a microcosm of life, containing many plant and insect species and as an important component of the food chain might symbolically signify fecundity.

However the turf was perceived, an equally important factor is that barrow construction engineered change in the surrounding landscape. Through modern eyes it might be interpreted in commercial terms or considered in a purely pragmatic manner, that is, a reduction in the availability of material needed for construction or fuel. Grazing land might be expected to be valued and the changes locally would only serve to increase restriction. One possibility is that the turf was newly cleared from areas needed for cultivation and heaped up as a ceremonial act of contrition for disturbing the earth.

Thus the function of long barrows is no easy matter to resolve. In addition, during the course of several manifestations over perhaps half a millennium, perceptions, beliefs and uses may have altered. Equally, it might be that the different forms of barrow played different roles. The extent to which primary use revolved around burial is uncertain and animal bones appear to have received similar treatment to those of human. As in Christian churches, use as burial places may have been just part of the story.

In addition to providing clues about settlement and territorial units, the locations chosen might offer some indications about belief. Construction on slightly sloping ground and on pervious soils implies either topographic constraints or a preoccupation with drainage. Traditional Chinese belief in the placing of tombs, for example, aims to ensure adequate drainage of the supernatural life force *c'hi* and thus the slope itself is of importance. That is not to say that long barrows were located with that in mind, but of all ancient monuments, barrows are likely to reflect something of belief in funereal matters and it is important not to place western 'Christian' preconceptions on their interpretation. The consistency of chosen location suggests that siting was not without purpose and that the link signals an association with important natural places in the landscape. The pit beneath some provides the first visible intervention in the land and signals the importance of the location. Whether these pits held posts or deposits of domestic debris can only be guessed at, but reports of D-shaped examples encourages the view that some at least once held timber uprights. If post or stone hole, the site may have marked an actual event. When excavated, the pit filling has invariably proved relatively clean of artefacts, as though any former use was reworked, the pit cleaned out and backfilled with fresh material. In some cases, it might be the result of misinterpretation by antiquaries, but in others it might hint at preparation for a new phase of use. It may be that beliefs, rituals and ceremonies moved on and it marks a period of change.

Research in Portugal has indicated that standing stones are amongst the earliest of monument types in Iberia and it may also be true of Brittany (Calado 2002). That many are incorporated into monuments in Brittany, for example, the well-known Table de Marchard and Gavrinis, but also Er Grah, Mané-Rutual, Mané-er-Hroëk, Mané Lud, implies that they played an early and central role in the creation of these monuments. Some of them were heavily reworked; some by being broken up and re-incorporated into the fabric, in one case built into two different monuments (see Bradley 2002).

A similar process may have taken place in Wiltshire. We are accustomed to the re-cutting of ditches and construction of new elements at causewayed enclosures, but similar changes may have taken place at long barrows as well. Cunnington specifically mentioned that the stones forming the cairn at Knook were 'large man made stones'. In Wiltshire, these can only have been deliberately broken sarsens, easily distinguished from natural boulders. It may be that these were broken from large stones that once stood alongside, given the position of the Arn Hill standing stone adjacent to the pavement. The pit discovered in a similar position at Knook may even have supported the stone.

It is difficult to be certain of the length of time between abandonment of the earliest 'ritual' pit, if that is the right term, and the next phase of activity. Evidence at a number of sites suggests that the façade and mortuary structures were almost or absolutely contemporary and at Haddenham and Skendleby, at least, the facade appears to have been a free-standing arrangement. Pavements are almost always placed adjacent to pits, not only providing an association between the two, but confirming the importance of that precise spot in the landscape. Pavements appear to have been constructed to take bodies or at least bones. Phillips (1936) and others have commented on how they were confined to the platform and not scattered beyond it and it may be that there was some retaining feature, a fence or hurdle, for otherwise bones might be dislodged by animal or other activity.

The bayed or cellular arrangements in some barrows incorporated sites both with and without burials. In many, the filling of these bays went on to form the bulk of the mound, but at some sites the post and stake hole layout suggests that it was the primary purpose of the monument. Although the point of it is not immediately apparent, it would appear that a function of the arrangement was to receive the materials from the ditch placed alongside. Should it simply be the earth itself that was important, it could be obtained in other ways, for example, by stripping one large area. The neatly stacked and ordered materials in each bay imply an order to the extraction similar to an archaeological spoil dump that has to be replaced. It may be that the ditches themselves were of importance and in terms of accumulation of debris those excavated at South Street seem to have been kept remarkably clean. Ditches can be important to hinder passage either for defensive or other practical reasons. But they might also hinder passage for supernatural elements and indeed it may be that the ditches were intended to insure that bad spirits became bogged down and could not enter the cellular area.

It seems that it was important to obtain earth and subsoil from alongside the fencing and the extraction of this was closely linked to the deposition. Assuming piecemeal or incremental activity, however, the ditch would not be considered as an entity until it was finished. And of course if the construction of cells was a progressive process, it may never have reached that point, work on it was simply interrupted and, for whatever reason, not restarted. Given this scenario, ditch digging would be a series of incrementally dug pits, each reflecting the material placed in an adjacent compartment. The placing of ditches either side of an axial fence, however, tends to imply that it is the central area that is of the greater importance, with the ditches acting as a quarry for materials, even if it is perceived in a supernatural manner. The axes are broadly ranged between midsummer and midwinter sunrises, or the reverse for lunar activity and the geometry is dominated by these alignments. The fence, at least, appears to be keyed in to events happening in the world about. In some cases, it may be that it marked a land boundary, either between settlements or types of land-use. As noted above a number of long barrows are thought to have been constructed at the edge of cultivated areas or on them as at South Street. But the fence is not merely of cosmological significance, for the offsets and sarsen boulders appear to be an integral part of the arrangement and they make no sense in terms of celestial alignments.

Alternatively, it may be that the bays relate to the individuals of a group or settlement. If so, the piecemeal manner in which the process was apparently extended implies that few individuals began the process. It could be that each bay represents an event, perhaps a calendrical one, when the earth was symbolically extracted and heaped into what would be an altar type arrangement. Perhaps ceremony was performed on or around as the material was extracted. Ultimately, the feature speaks of change, for each mini-event involves changing the environment. There is no evidence for a lengthy period of activity and it may equally be, as was pointed out at Giant's Hills 2, that such a process could take no more than a few months.

There is often evidence of destruction. A small turf mound was placed at the east end of the mortuary structure at Haddenham, effectively blocking it. This was almost a miniature version of the round mound that blocked the entrance to the mortuary enclosure at Wor Barrow. It was subsequently partly destroyed and the façade dismantled (Hodder and Shand 1988, 352). Radiocarbon dates indicate that perhaps two centuries after construction, the façade at Skendleby 2 was burnt down. Only then were the human bones placed between the posts in the mortuary structure and the mound built over them. At Nutbane, the first forecourt structure was removed to allow for a second larger structure, over which the primary mound was built leaving the façade standing proud, but this was subsequently burnt leaving the secondary mound to be erected around the burning posts.

Deposits of 'occupation debris' or 'midden material' often occur in various positions within and around the mound, at Skendleby, for example, being deposited at the east end outside the revetment trench and at the heart of the monument sealing the pit and stone 'wall'. It was considered to have been brought from elsewhere and placed in position. Phillips considered that it must have been ritually deposited and there are other indications that he may have been correct in his judgement. Midden material interleaved with clean rubble was used to fill the chamber at West Kennet (Piggott 1962a), while the lack of human bones in chambered cairns on the Isles of Scilly led Paul Ashbee (1976) to suggest that they may be repositories for the 'occupation earth' or settlement debris that was found in them. Suggesting that the deposits of soil and broken pottery filling the chambers was comparable to the material found in some of the chambers in Scotland and in long barrows and causewayed enclosures, he considered that there may have been a perceived association between settlement debris and plant development and growth. Problems regarding soil fertility were almost certainly recognised and these monuments may be a response to that. If they were repositories containing a symbolic deposit of soil and settlement debris, an initial foundation deposit might be added to incrementally.

Our modern perception of refuse as rubbish is in fact quite a recent one. Until the turn of the nineteenth to twentieth century most 'waste' was recycled, often through the hands of a small army of sifters and distributors. Collections were introduced to primarily assist in getting rid of ash from towns, gathering of the 'dust' being made by 'dustmen' and 'dustcarts' (see for example Eedle 1971). Formerly the manuring effect of 'waste' as distinct from the contribution made by stock was more widely appreciated and may well have had an extremely long history. Weathered Bronze Age potsherds found widely scattered during archaeological fieldwalking are often put down to manuring practice, especially where found in areas of 'Celtic' fields. However, at East Chisenbury, in Wiltshire a massive mound of refuse some 180m in diameter and at least 2.5m high, comprising settlement debris, animal bones, broken pottery, spindlewhorls, etc., all dating to the latest Bronze Age and earliest Iron Age, appears to have been curated. Far from being put out on the fields, it was heaped into a mound of monumental proportions on the summit of the hillside away from the expected foci of settlement. The reason for this is by no means clear, but analysis of just a small sample of the debris reveals that, if scaled up, it represents the consumption of 3800 sheep and 600 cattle annually over a 100-year period, some thing far beyond the capability of a local farmstead (McOmish *et al.* 2002). The debris is therefore likely to result from meat eating and other activities representing conspicuous consumption on an enormous scale. The point of this is not to suggest that all debris was symbolic, but that it could be treated in a very different way to that expected.

THE CHANGING ROLE OF LONG BARROWS

Few long barrows were constructed after the end of the fourth millennium and beliefs and practices involving their use seem to have been modified. No secondary burials of this period have been recorded and aside from the occasional visits during which the above material was deposited, the monuments appear to have been treated in a different manner. If the lozenge-shaped flint arrowheads found near the west end of Winterbourne Stoke 35 (Thurnam 1864)

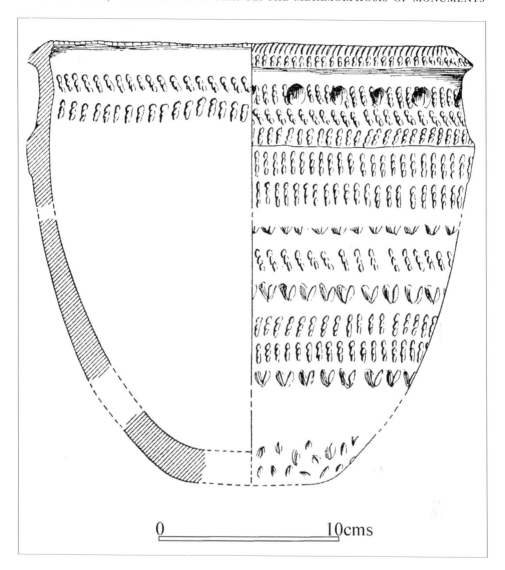

67 Reconstructed Mortlake Ware bowl from the secondary ditch deposits at Badshot Lea long barrow. *After Keiller and Piggott 1939*

can be compared to those in the Seamer hoard, itself relying on a single date of C14 determination of 3500-2900 cal. BC (HAR 5587) from the Whitegrounds cairn, the crouched burial which they accompanied might date from this time. The twin crouched burial at Abingdon with their simple grave goods, may be of similar date based on the radiocarbon dates from the ditches, as might, broadly, that at Alfriston, where antler from the ditch provided a date of 3350-2550 cal. BC (HAR-940). The four lozenge arrowheads found in Pistle Barrow could also be of this date. All of these sites are relatively small barrows containing single grave pits with articulated skeletons (Thorpe 1984) and it is worth recalling the suggestions that oval barrows may be later than others (Drewett 1986: Barrett *et al.* 1991, 51-3).

Mortlake Ware bowls with a date range of from 3400-2500 cal. BC were found in secondary ditch deposits in both ditches at Badshot Lea along with red deer, pig and cattle bones (*67*). Bone from the north ditch provided a date for the event of 3700-2900 cal. BC (BM-2272). Mortlake Ware was found in similar secondary and upper ditch deposits at Wor Barrow, at North Marden, as well as at Skendleby 2, where although at least two pots were present, neither was complete. They do not appear to have been accidentally broken on site and left behind; on the contrary like some of the earlier pottery found at long barrows, they seem to have been deliberately deposited. The blade end of a broken ground-flint axe was found in the same levels at Badshot Lea (*68*) and another in a similar position at Wor Barrow. Considerable amounts of flint debitage were also recovered from secondary ditch deposits at Easton Down (Whittle *et al.* 1993). Material is frequently found on the surface around barrows and the blade and butt end of ground axes were both recovered from this position at Horslip, while ground axes occurred amongst surface material at Alfriston (Drewett 1975, fig 12). However, Paul Ashbee commented that while flakes were found on the surface surrounding the mound at Fussell's Lodge, the greatest concentration occurred *on it*.

In the third millennium there was a greater move towards the use of round barrows. This was hardly a new innovation given the circular mounds beneath Wor Barrow, Old Ditch and elsewhere, but it is simply that a certain element of the architectural repertoire was preferred. Having covered the circular structure at Wor Barrow with earth, two small round barrows, Handley 26 and 27, were constructed immediately adjacent. In Yorkshire, round barrows frequently occur, but they are by no means absent in the south (Kinnes 1979), for example the small mound at Mere 13d or on Therfield Heath (*colour plate 29*), and it may be that some of the round mounds in southern cemeteries are in fact of this date.

The area around the South Street long barrow appears to have undergone dramatic changes during the middle of the third millennium BC. Little more than 200m away an oval enclosure, 140 x 110m, was constructed which has recently been investigated by Joshua Pollard, Mark Gillings and Dave Wheatley. It comprised a narrow, 2.1m wide and at 1m deep, relatively shallow interrupted ditch with bank placed on the inside. The excavators considered that cattle and pig bone coupled with decorated potsherds found along the ditch might be interpreted as the remains of feasts, but there was a lack of internal features and the function of the enclosure remains unclear. Some time after construction,

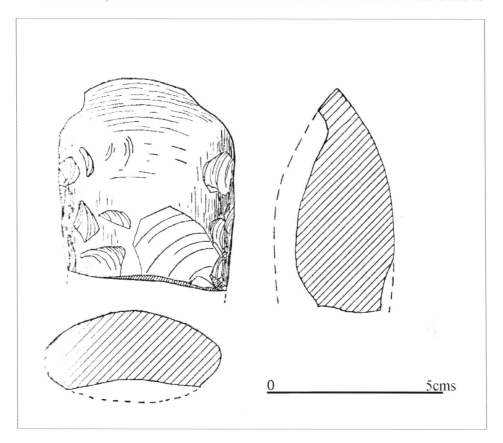

68 Ground-flint axe blade found in the secondary ditch deposits at Badshot Lea long barrow.
After Keiller and Piggott 1939

the bank was levelled (Pollard and Reynolds 2002). This may have been to accommodate the Beckhampton stone avenue, one of two that led into Avebury henge a little over 1km to the north-east. Whether the long barrow influenced the siting of these monuments is unclear. Although only a stones throw away, the course of the avenue completely ignores South Street, but at the very least it will have provided a visible reminder of ancestral presence, whoever the builders of these later monuments were.

In the latter part of the third millennium there was an increase in the incidence of visible burials in the archaeological record. In the Stonehenge area, burials accompanied by Beakers may have been marked on the surface in some way as the sites often received later burial deposits cut into or placed over a pre-existing grave. In one case, Wilsford cum Lake G52, there were nine successive inhumations and only at the end of a potentially lengthy sequence was a mound raised over them (Smith 1991). Some burials were placed in, or on, long mounds. At Wilsford 34, 500km south-east of the Winterbourne Stoke Crossroads barrow, Thurnam uncovered five secondary burials. One of which, in a crouched position had a Beaker adjacent to the hips. Three other crouched burials had no accompanying grave goods. Further crouched burials associated with Beakers were found at Winterbourne Stoke 35, and at Figheldean 31 (*69*), a little over 500m east of Robin Hood's Ball causewayed enclosure. The central part of the latter mound has since been removed and three large sarsens placed in the ditch, presumably by a local farmer (There are other sarsens in the vicinity and Cunnington noted that they are often ploughed up by local farmers).

Crouched burials lacking Beakers, but which *might* be attributed to the period were also found at Amesbury 42, at the eastern end of the Stonehenge cursus at Amesbury 14, to the south-west of Stonehenge, where Thurnam encountered three contracted skeletons with a third lying beneath one of the others and in the Winterbourne Stoke Crossroads long barrow, where six crouched skeletons of a male, female and several children, were found just 0.6m below the surface accompanied by a 'food vase' and flint knife (Thurnam 1869, 196-8).

The long barrows were evidently revered as an appropriate place for such burial of individuals. The high archaeological visibility of Beaker associated interments in contrast to those with Grooved Ware and other later Neolithic material highlights a potential difference in belief patterns. Later Neolithic burials are rare and this absence in the archaeological record serves to promote an implication that corpses from the greater part of the population were deposited in natural places, exposed on hilltops, trees or deposited in rivers. In contrast, the Beaker incorporation of bodies in long barrows not only indicates that there was some recognition that the mound was of significance, but also that it was deemed politically and ritually acceptable to use it in that way. Having established a new role, insertion of burials into long mounds, the practice appears to have continued, a little like the burials that focused on Christian churches during historic times.

At Skendleby 1, the complete skeleton of a two or three year old domestic cow was found in association with Beaker potsherds midway along the northernmost ditch. Given the interest in such mounds for burial it may have been a votive deposit. The Beaker sherds lay close to the spine of the animal, which lay on its left side with head towards the distal end of the barrow. Its skull survived in a damaged condition, although whether this was pre or post deposition in the barrow is not clear. Other cattle bones, as well as sheep, pig and dog remains, perhaps symbolic of the lifestyle, were present along with a certain amount of flint knapping debris, including a spall from a ground and highly-polished flint axe, and a miniature bronze awl. Deposition of such midden material continues the process begun much earlier and the mound may still have served some purpose in terms of renewal and regeneration.

69 Beaker from Figheldean 31 long barrow found accompanying a crouched skeleton. *Thurnam 1869*

Two fragments of Beaker were recovered from behind the revetment trench at Skendleby 1, sealed beneath a dump of loam that Phillips thought was turf. The sherds were weathered and he felt that they had been scooped up and incorporated with material from the surrounding land surface in the body of the barrow. The deposit was also sealed by chalk, which, if from the ditch implies that the Beaker sherds were present before the ditch was dug. The presence of Beaker in such a position is difficult to account for. Perhaps the easiest explanation is that the sherds fell down a root hole or were dragged down an animal burrow, although there is no indication of such an occurrence in the excavation illustrations. If accepted at face value it might imply that the mound or at least the eastern end of it was not constructed until a relatively late date.

Beaker-related activity around these monuments was by no means entirely funerary in nature. At South Street, a clearance horizon containing Beaker potsherds at the eastern end of the southern ditch revealed criss-cross plough-marks. Cultivation had evidently taken place across the ditch and up to the edge of the mound. Astonishingly it lay on the same north to south orientation as the plough-marks in the pre-barrow soil and raises the intriguing possibility that remnants of the Neolithic fields were visible as earthworks or hedgerows allowing them to be reworked. Elsewhere the presence of sherds found in the upper ditch silts at, for example, Skendleby 2, North Marden, Fussell's Lodge, Abingdon and West Rudham may derive from similar activities, as in some cases, at Nutbane, Kilham, and Horslip they are found in association with a dark loam soil deposit thought to represent a ploughsoil.

BRONZE AGE

Fascination with old sites continued in the Bronze Age and beyond. The fact that the site had been covered in earth may have added a sense of mystery, or perhaps there was still some memory of the former use, with traditions, stories and a sense of relationship to those whose bones were now beyond inspection. Or perhaps the mound itself simply remained an important focal point within the landscape. There was no more ditch re-cutting, or tidying up, simply deposits of pottery and midden-like material perhaps symbolically left in the ditch.

The deposition of secondary burials continued. Cunnington found a cremation on a cinerary urn in a secondary position in the mound at Corton, while, towards the east end of King Barrow, he recovered a 'prettily ornamented' urn that he thought might have contained a secondary cremation and which had in turn been disturbed by later insertions. A bipartite urn was found near the surface in Oxendean long barrow (70), while two secondary cremations were close to the surface at Old Ditch. One was dispersed by the excavators before Cunnington could check it, the other with several fragments of skull and teeth recognisable, was placed in a 'cist' or small depression 'not larger than the crown of a small hat'. Thurham also often recorded the presence of secondary material including burials, usually in 'the upper strata or near the summits.' (Thurnam 1869, 195-7).

In some cases, the mound itself was adapted. One of two crouched inhumation burials accompanied by food vessels at Kilham, lay beneath a circular

70 Early Bronze Age vessel, a secondary insertion at Oxendean Down long barrow.
Thurnam 1869

mound situated on the west end of the long barrow, while a ring ditch was also constructed over a post avenue at the east end. A round barrow was also built on the eastern end of the long mound at Beckhampton Road, a portion of an urn and a barbed and tanged arrowhead being attributed to it. It may be that other long mounds also had round barrows constructed in that position. The swelling at the east end of White Barrow may be a case in point, as may those 'pyriform' examples that Stukeley observed at a time when many were in better condition.

Chronology can also be detected in the area immediately surrounding barrows and there are some well-known examples that form the focus of a developing barrow cemetery; Winterbourne Stoke Crossroads, for example, where the axis of the long barrow has been echoed and adapted by a series of later mounds or Therfield Heath where barrows are camouflaged by golf earthworks. On Normanton Down, a small long barrow was subsequently dwarfed by the massive, bell and disc barrows around it, while at Lake nearby, some 21 round barrows are bracketed on the uphill slope by a long barrow. Some of this nucleation may result from lack of space in the surrounding countryside. Embryonic fields were

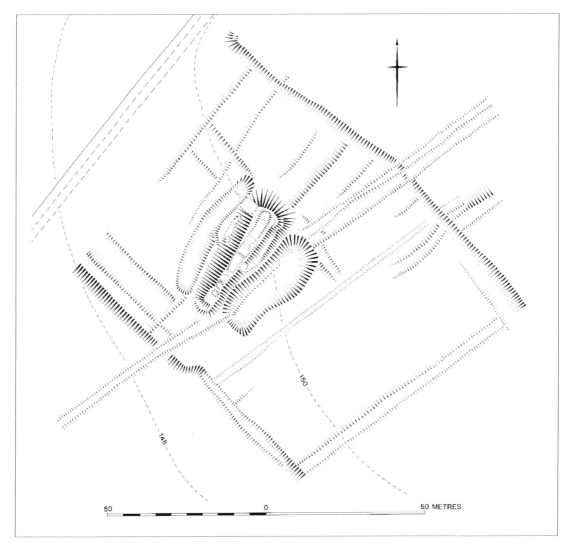

71 Plan of Fittleton long barrow, Wiltshire showing the encroachment of 'Celtic' fields and later features. © *Crown copyright NMR*

laid out adjacent to the Beaker settlement site on Easton Down and we have already seen that Beaker cultivation was carried across the long barrow ditch at South Street. At Hopton Street, Southwark, there was a compressed use of space that squeezed cultivation close between structures and the edge of the River Thames (Ridgeway 1999: 74), while evidence of Beaker-period cultivation in liminal environments can also be found at Rosinish, Outer Hebrides (Shepherd 1976: Shepherd and Tuckwell 1977) and at Gwithian, in Cornwall (Simpson 1971: Megaw 1976).

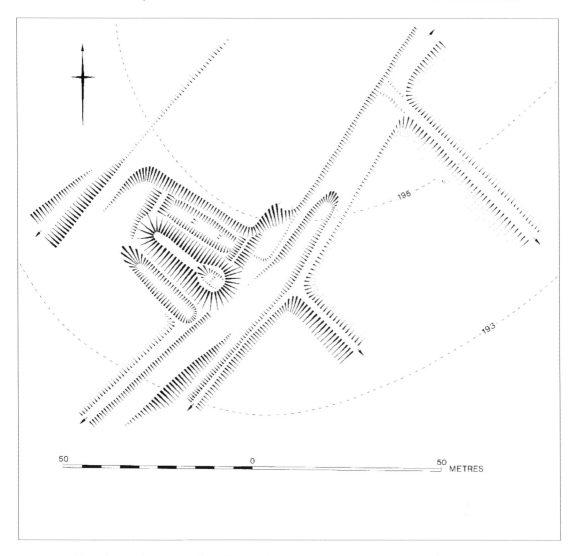

72 Plan of Oxendean Down long barrow showing encroachment by 'Celtic' fields. © *Crown copyright NMR*

Towards the middle of the second millennium BC new land-units were laid out co-axially across large areas in some parts of the countryside. Bronze Age fields encroach on Fittleton long barrow (*71*), Middleton Down, Netheravon 6, Oxendean (*72*) and Kill Barrow, and may be responsible for modification of the mounds, obscuring one of the ditches in the latter case. An episode of cultivation is present at Nutbane, where ploughsoil in the upper levels of the ditch contained Deverel Rimbury pottery and there may also have been Middle Bronze Age cultivation at Giant's Hills 2, Skendleby. At a later date, around the

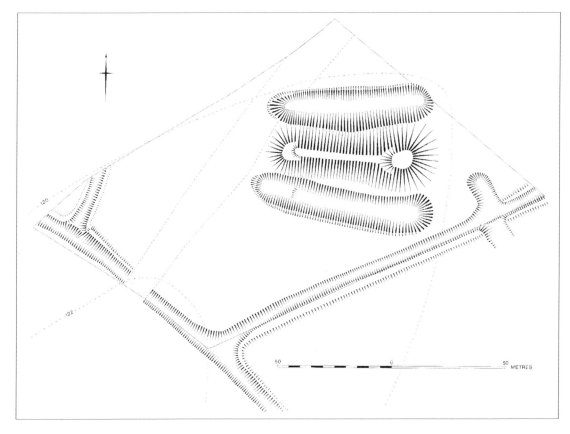

73 Plan of White Barrow showing isolation by a series of Later Bronze Age linear ditches.
© *Crown copyright NMR*

turn of the second to first millennium BC, a further dramatic change occurred on large parts of the chalkland hills. The land was subdivided into a series of parish boundary or tithing-like units by a system of linear ditches that laid out for kilometres across the countryside. In so doing, they often cut across old fields, putting them out of use. Many of these linear ditches incorporated long barrows into their course at, for example, Old Ditch, Kill Barrow and White Barrow (73), in each case focusing on and modifying the appearance of the monuments.

The human impact on the countryside during the Iron Age is sometimes difficult to detect. The climate steadily worsened and this may have discouraged cultivation on the higher ground. The large prominent barrow on Hambledon Hill was enclosed by a series of massive ramparts, but no others were treated in this way. If visited, the excavation record on any activity remains silent

ROMAN

Many long mounds were revisited during the first half of the first millennium AD and there appears to have been some recognition of their former significance. At Jullieberrie's Grave, three inhumations were recorded on the southern edge of the ditch, while a fourth, a partial skeleton, had a pot with it containing what was thought to be the rest of the body. They were associated with eight late fourth-century coins, a bronze bracelet, a bronze brooch and pottery vessels along with animal remains, presumably the residue of a feast (Jessup 1939).

The mound on White Horse Hill, Uffington, formed the focus for a large number of burials; altogether there were 46 skeletons buried in 42 graves. Five of the individuals had coins in their mouths, which dated them to the late Roman-period. Partial re-excavation and geophysical surveys in June 1993 demonstrated that the cemetery extends for an unknown distance around the long barrow (Miles and Palmer 1993). Many of the skeletons lacked skulls.

Similar headless bodies were inserted into Wor Barrow (74), where of seventeen Romano-British burials found in the mound and ditch, eight were minus their heads and one of these also had the feet cut off. Four headless skeletons were also found below the turf on the summit of the mound at Knook and although no dating evidence was produced by Cunnington it seems likely that they were Romano-British in date.

Similar material has been found in other long barrows. At Skendleby 1, a coin of Allectus AD 293-6 found in the ditch is associated with a return of the local landscape to grassland (Cecil in Phillips 1936, 103). In fact, the deposition of coins appears to have been quite frequent and it may be that like those deposited in the ditch at Silbury Hill, they represent spiritual offerings. Whether the hoard

74 Secondary interments at Wor Barrow with severed skulls. *From Pitt Rivers 1898*

of Constantinian coins found in a pot while digging for a fence in the early nineteenth-century at Jullieberrie's Grave was such an offering or whether they were deposited for safekeeping is uncertain (Jessup 1939).

SAXON

In contrast to the execution victims placed in long barrows during the Romano-British period, a number of richly furnished warrior burials occur with effect from the late sixth or early seventh century. Whether this was the result of traditions and belief imported from the continent or whether they were inserted into such places in order to make a political point to the indigenous population is not clear (Eagles and Field 2004).

When excavated by Richard C. Hoare, Pentridge 23, a long barrow located immediately west of Bokerley Dyke and a short distance north of the north-eastern terminal of the Dorset Cursus, a rich seventh-century Anglo-Saxon burial was revealed. Hoare reported the discovery of an extended female inhumation placed on what is thought to be a bed-like structure. With it were a biconical gold bead, two glass beads, one of them threaded on a gold wire ring, a jet bead, and a millefiori plaque suspended from a gold chain thought to represent the remains of a necklace. Also present were iron objects, a small hook, a buckle and a clench bolt, and an ivory ring, some of which were thought to be fittings of the bed (Hoare 1812, 235).

More frequently such burials are associated with weaponry. A skeleton at King Barrow had a sword at its thigh and a spearhead and ferrule accompanied a skeleton at Therfield Heath (Phillips 1935), while at Lyneham, Oxfordshire, excavations in 1894 located two Anglo-Saxon burials inserted into the summit of the mound, one with a spearhead and knife, the other with a knife. Of three secondary skeletons all lying east to west at Sherrington, one 'a very stout man' was accompanied by a sword, knife, spearhead, shield boss and other objects (75). The others, an adult and a young child of four to five were accompanied by a small knife and a piece of lead. The sex of the second adult was unrecorded, but the presence of the child introduces the intriguing possibility that it was a family group. A fourth burial was discovered elsewhere in the barrow with a spearhead on its right side (Eagles and Field 2004). Two crouched secondary Saxon inhumations were found at Tilshead, Wiltshire. Hoare and Cunnington excavated an unaccompanied skeleton lying west to east just beneath the turf near the east end, but when Thurnam reopened the barrow at the centre, he encountered an extended skeleton just below the surface. This had its head to the west, and was accompanied by the remains of a wooden bucket bound with thin straps of bronze and, the handle, studs and boss, of a shield.

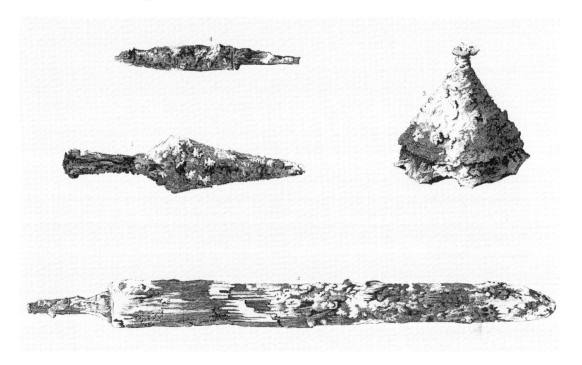

75 Iron sword, spearhead, knife and spear boss found with secondary interments at Sherrington Barrow, Wiltshire. *From Lambert 1806*

As in the Romano-British period, some mounds became the focus for larger numbers of burials. Indeed, some such as Uffington appear to have continued in use as a cemetery (Miles and Palmer 1993, 22). An inhumation cemetery dating from the ninth century was revealed at Bevis' Grave, overlooking Portsmouth Harbour. The mound was thought to have been first opened in 1815 when three skeletons were found close to the surface, one with a broken spear lying at the side. More recent excavations by David Rudling, revealed over 80 Anglo-Saxon burials set around the south-east corner of the barrow and alongside the ditch and associated with grave goods including knives and buckles. Most were aligned east to west and were thought to be Christian burials (Anon 1974, 23; Anon 1975, 92-3). In the north, excavations by Tim Brewster during the 1960s at Kemp Howe, Cottam, Humberside, revealed twelve Anglo-Saxon inhumations found in narrow graves, five of them in coffins and dating to the middle of the eighth century AD. Like those at Bevis' Grave they were thought to be Christian and were set into the ditch of an oval barrow that surmounted the east end of the long barrow (Anon 1968, 30).

CHARTERS

The number of Christian burials in long mounds comes as something of a surprise and raises questions concerning the extent to which traditional values and customs were retained during this transitory period. Following the struggle between beliefs there were few additions to barrows. Nevertheless the mounds appear to have been recognised as important focal points within the landscape. A number of late Saxon land charters used mounds to help define their estate boundaries.

Adam's Grave, Wiltshire, has been identified with the Wodnesbeorge of a charter of AD 825, while Boles Barrow, Bodelusburgge (Grindy 1920, 82) was mentioned in a charter of AD 968; and yet the long mound at Brixton Deverill, Wiltshire, is simply referred to as 'lang beorh' in a Saxon charter. Other mounds were frequently incorporated into land unit boundaries, much as they had been in the Later Bronze Age. Lambourne long barrow, for example, west of the Seven Barrows cemetery, lies on the boundaries of Kingston Lisle, Lambourn and Sparsholt parishes.

They may thus have been of peripheral importance to the developing social units; though nevertheless of interest regarding the personal names applied to some just 200-300 years after the insertion of the secondary burials, and perhaps not long enough for folk memory to have entirely extinguished. Whether the stout individual with a sword blow to the skull found in Ell Barrow was the individual of the place-name, or one of the secondary burials found in Boles Barrow was the Bodelus mentioned in the tenth-century charter from which the mound gets its name is unknown. But essentially the mounds were forgotten and by the end of the Middle Ages they could only be recalled as part of myth and tradition, and were considered pagan places unsuitable for Christian folk (76). The long barrow at Sprotborough, South Yorkshire is known as Hengist's Grave, two mounds along the south coast are named after 'Bevis', but mounds elsewhere, at for example, Downton, Luckington, and Milton Lilborne, became the graves of 'giants' or the site of poorly remembered battles. According to tradition, Slaughter Barrow at Gillingham in Dorset was the burial place of those who were killed during a conflict between the Danish and Saxon armies in 1016, the link presumably deriving from the proximity of the village of Penn, where a battle was fought between Edmund Ironside and Canute (Warne 1866, 50). There were similar accounts of a battle at Lanhill. According to Aubrey, the mound was known as Hubba's-Lowe, referring to a Danish leader who died during a battle with the Saxons close to the site.

76 Combe Gibbet long barrow, Inkpen Beacon, Berkshire. Replaced in the early 1950s, the gibbet is thought to have been the third on the site, the pagan mound being considered an appropriate place for criminals to be hung

FINALE

Following the valley of the River Till upstream past Winterbourne Stoke, to the west of Stonehenge, reveals a hidden valley, sheltered from the elements and comfortably enclosed by the subtly weathered chalk hills round about. The stream winds through the downs twisting from one flank to the other in order to absorb the fluvial contribution from each re-entrant coombe in turn. Several villages of medieval origin focus on the stream, Winterbourne Stoke itself, Shrewton, Maddington, Elston, Orcheston. All of these villages utilised the valley slopes for agriculture, though beyond these cultivated areas, prehistoric and Romano-British earthworks survive. Now the stream is seasonal, the water being extracted in great quantities and, like elsewhere, subsistence relies on piped water. Formerly it was rather different and several houses built at Shrewton and Orcheston have notices reminding passers-by that a number of dwellings were destroyed by a great flood in 1841 testifying to the one-time power of the water. At Tilshead, nothing is to be seen of it apart from during exceptionally wet periods. On such occasions springs bubble up and pools coalesce into a slither of running water. Here the valley and its associated coombes are narrow, the floor being occupied by the string of houses of Tilshead village. Within the immediate vicinity are six long barrows, mostly situated on the narrow interfluves above the coombe floors. Following one such bottom north-west of the village, the passage is periodically boggy except where a modern ditch has been cut to channel the water. The coombe slopes provide definition to the place and limits to the visible world, while trees along the flanks provide character and tell of former land-use. As the terminal to the valley approaches, the gradient increases and there, proud against the skyline, is Kill Barrow, in silhouette like a prone animal. The contours of the valley lead directly to the mound leaving no doubt in the mind that the two are linked. At 39m in length, Kill Barrow is just an average-sized long barrow (*77*). It is still 2m in height, yet approached from all sides, but that said, appears quite undistinguished and unnoticeable. Indeed, little more than 100m to the west it is out of sight.

When Thurnam excavated here in 1865 he found that:

> several bodies had been burnt very imperfectly, some of the bones being merely charred. Others were stained a brilliant green and blue, but chemical tests yielded no traces of copper. Under a pile of a white friable substance like half-dried shelly mortar, were curious masses of a sort of ossiferous breccia; the burnt human bones, black, white, blue and green, being closely cemented by calcareous matter.

He noted in his catalogue that:

> The primary interment consisted of piles of burnt bones on the floor of the barrow at the east end. One of these to the east of the other, would have filled about a peck; the other 6ft or 7ft nearer the middle of the barrow, was in much greater quantity. These burnt bones were some of them curiously (Mixed) with burnt flints, sarsen chips, etc., into what I have called an ossiferous breccia, and many were stained vivid blue and green colour. These burnt bones were unequally burnt, and many merely charred were quite black. Above the bones the chalk rubble of the barrow was curiously changed into a delicate friable cream-coloured substance like burnt shells. I fancy this an imperfect lime, formed probably from the burnt bones having been deposited whilst hot. This substance was very abundant, and would probably have filled a bushel.

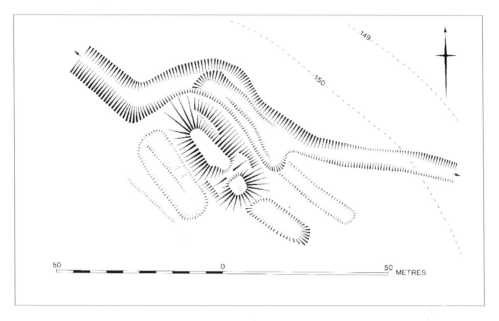

77 Plan of Kill Barrow showing the linear ditch that skirts the mound, utilising the north-east ditch before cutting downslope towards Tilshead. © *Crown copyright NMR*

Other than this there is no indication of the internal components of the mound, or whether there was a pavement or burial chamber. For the rest of the Neolithic, the record is silent.

At some point, probably in the Middle Bronze Age, a system of small square (rectangular) fields was laid out across the down, both on the slopes of the River Till, below the barrow and across the ridge into the valley beyond (*colour plate 30*). Who farmed these fields is not exactly clear but they probably represent the changing agrarian regime of a community that already occupied the hillside and coombe, and may have done so for many generations. The enclosed fields marked a change in the way that the land was used, being parcelled out to distinguish between different uses or users. The long barrow no longer appears to have played a role, although as it was not levelled its relevance to earlier generations may have been respected.

Perhaps 500 years later, after the fields on the slope had developed lynchets, the community faced a further challenge. The catalyst is unknown. It may have been a response to the changing climate but it was a practice widely adopted across the chalk downland at this time. The land was divided by long and wide ditches, linear ditches, which carved out parish or tithing-like territories from valley to hillside. Like the nearby long barrows, Old Ditch and White Barrow, Kill Barrow was used as a pivotal marker in laying out the new system. The ditch snaked across the summit of the down across to the southernmost ditch of the barrow but carefully changed direction, curved around the north-west end of the barrow to utilise the northernmost ditch, exiting at the eastern end before turning east and leading obliquely downslope, making slight sinuous turns every time that it cut through a field boundary. There is some hint that a different course was planned in terms of a shallow continuation of the line of the long barrow ditch, although so much twentieth-century military interference here makes the earthworks particularly difficult to disentangle. At one point approximately 200m to the east, the ditch makes a series of dramatic turns, evidently intended to avoid some important feature that existed in the contemporary landscape. Two circular depressions among the 'Celtic' fields hint at the possibility of a homestead. The new land division effectively put a large number of fields out of use and presumably indicates a complete change in the method of land-use, perhaps large-scale cattle ranching, or more likely, given the results from the nearby Late Bronze Age midden at East Chisenbury, sheep walks on a scale that almost matched those of the historic period. Such activity may have relieved pressure on the long mound, the only damage being a result of livestock traversing the earthwork.

The barrow provided a guide post for tracks crossing the interior of the almost tree less Salisbury Plain and a major Roman route developed just to the south-west of the site. Like other Roman settlements, this probably began by utilising a pre-existing Late Bronze Age linear ditch, which sinuously followed the false crest of the valley to the south. Compounds containing probable hut stances flank the road and are superimposed upon and at a different angle to the earlier 'Celtic' field system. The settlement therefore appears to have something to do with the road system, rather than being agriculturally based and while some of the fields might have been brought back into use in a small way, this lack of interest probably resulted in the survival of the long barrow, not to mention demise of the village. Elsewhere on Salisbury Plain, agriculturally based fields were heavily ploughed during the Romano-British period and the landscape engineered to such an extent that lynchets up to 7m in height have been recorded. Such settlements almost certainly will have destroyed earlier monuments. How the barrow was considered by the local community is not known – it was lucky.

Like the other villages out on the downs, the settlement at Chapperton Down appears to have become largely deserted, but may have lingered on into the early fifth century AD, after which land-use and tenurial links become uncertain until the historical use of charters in the ninth and tenth centuries. Two secondary burials were placed in the mound, both with head to the north. Neither of the burials appears to have had distinguishing grave goods and they could be of almost any period. The frequency with which Anglo-Saxon burials were made in other local barrows implies that they may be of that age too. Whether they represented people living on the down nearby, or in the valley at Tilshead is not clear.

The long barrow had acquired its own name, Gyllebarow from at least 1461 when it was first mentioned in documents, and probably very much earlier. The monument remained a marker for shepherds and travellers crossing the down between Tilshead and Imber and trackways crossing the ridge at this point are still evident. Cultivation was probably not reintroduced until the post-medieval period. The ridge and furrow that can be seen utilizing the earthen boundaries left by the 'Celtic' field enclosures was shallow and probably short lived, perhaps in response to a period of high corn prices. If not completely levelled by the 'Celtic' fields it may have been this that all but obscured the southernmost of Kill Barrow's ditches, although it was not serious enough to affect the mound itself.

During the First World War the mound, unlike that at nearby Knook, narrowly escaped destruction, as a trench system and live bombardment area destroyed part of the Romano British settlement to the west. A threat of recent years has been from tanks, as several squadrons at a time would charge the ridge, although a well-considered tree planting regime has now diverted this activity. Now as with other mounds on the chalk downland, the major threat is from burrowing animals, rabbits and badgers, from which even the well-known long barrow at Winterbourne Stoke Crossroads has not escaped. Formerly rabbits were caught in large numbers on Salisbury Plain and sent to market, 14,000 in one year from a single estate, but now there are no predators and unfortunately barrows make fine warrens.

It may be that with time and further discoveries barrows, both long and round, will provide us with much more data than that relating to prehistoric burial rites and material culture, not that these are unimportant. Increasing numbers of mortuary enclosures and new types of allied site are changing the distribution pattern and it is apparent that the prehistoric landscape was more densely occupied than once thought. From this it is evident that barrows were not peripheral but at the heart of the British landscape, providing an ancestral focus around which settlement and other activities have been framed.

As in the case of Kill Barrow, the extant long barrows are accidents of survival, the result of diminished agricultural opportunities, for whatever reason. The twentieth century changed all that. Even now the plough is encroaching on a number of barrows and others are continually under cultivation and their mounds will soon disappear.

The value of the surviving barrows lies not merely in their nature as depositories of archaeological material. Even in their denuded and turf covered state, we can see the effect that they must have had in the landscape and envisage their influence on both lives and land-use. They will have marked out and punctuated the countryside, signposting locations of tradition and ancestral importance, just as churches did for the historic period and, like the churches, they will have signalled a spiritual message and provided an entry to the supernatural that provided comfort to the community in its struggle to reproduce.

APPENDIX

SELECTED RADIOCARBON DATES

Previously published dates reproduced here have been substantiantially supported by those derived from the CBA Database of Radiocarbon dates and calibrated using the OxCal3.9 programme. Several long barrows, Fussell's Lodge, West Kennet, Waylands Smithy, Whiteleaf and Ascott-under-Wychwood along with the Hazleton long cairn have now been provided with date models based on Bayesian analysis. Refer to Bayliss & Whittle 2007 and Hey *et al* 2007 for details of these.

Site	Lab No	Feature	Material	BP	Cal. BC
DORSET					
Wor Barrow	BM2283R	Ditch primary	Antler	4660+/-130	3700-3000
	BM-2284R	Ditch primary	Antler	4740+/-130	3800-3050
Thickthorn Down	BM-2355	Buried soil	Antler	5160+/-45	4040-4200 4040-3900 3880-3800
Allington Avenue, Dorset	HAR-8579	Ditch primary fill	Bone	4450+/-80	3351-2920
GLOUCESTER					
Hazleton North	OxA-383	South chamber	Human bone	4450+/-90	3361-2911
KINCARDINE					
Dalladies	I-6113	Mortuary structure, phase 2	Charred wood	5190+/-105	4319-3768
	SRR-289	Mortuary structure, phase 2	Charred wood	4660+/-50	3630-3352
	SRR-290	Mortuary structure, phase 2	Charred wood	4535+/-55	3491-3029
LINCOLNSHIRE					
Skendleby 2	OxA-641	Façade post	Charcoal	5450+/-80	4454-4054
	OxA-642	Façade post	Charcoal	5140+/-80	4227-3713
	CAR-821	Post pit	Charcoal	5100+/-100	4225-3658

	CAR-822	Post pit	Charcoal	4970+/-100	3975-3534
	OxA-639	Burial	Human skull	4650+/-80	3638-3109
	OxA-640	Burial	Human skull	4770+/-80	3695-3370
	CAR-819	Mound	Antler	4840+/-70	3776-3381
	CAR-820	Ditch	Antler	4800+/-80	3714-3371
Ulceby	BM-2750	Primary ditch silt	Antler	4660+/-60	3635-3340
NORTHAMPTONSHIRE					
Redlands Fm, Stanwick	OxA-5632	Primary phase	Human bone	4825+/-65	3761-3378
	OxA5633	Primary phase cist	Bone	4820+/-80	3768-3376
Aldwincle mortuary enclosure	HAR-1411	Inner ditch base	Charcoal	4560+/-70	3517-3027
	CAR-821	Post pit	Charcoal	4970+/-100	3975-3534
	CAR-819	Mound	Antler	4840+/- 70	3776-3381
	CAR-822	Mortuary area	Charcoal from post pit	4970+/-100	3975-3534
Raunds	OxA-3001	Ditch upper organic fill	Seeds	4810+/-80	3763-3373
	OxA-3003	Revetment collapse	Wood (oak)	4790+/-90	3761-3367
OXFORDSHIRE					
Barrow Hills, Abingdon	BM-3391	Primary ditch	Antler (red deer)		3370-3030 or 2975-2935
	BM-2393	Ditch filling	Antler		3340-3215 or 3195-2915
	BM-2390	Ditch filling	Antler		3350-2605
	BM-2391	Primary ditch phase 5	Antler		3330-3225 or 3185-3155 or 3145-2865 or 2810-2750 or 2725-2695 or 2675-2665
SURREY					
Badshot Lea	BM-2272	Secondary ditch	Bone	4640=/-130	3700-2900
	BM-2273	Primary ditch silt	Bone	4740=/-20	3640-3550 3540-3500 3430-3380

	BM-2274	Primary ditch silt	Antler (red deer)	4860+/-180	4045-3104
SUSSEX					
North Marden	HAR-5544	Secondary ditch silts		4710=/-110	3750-3100
Alfriston	HAR-940	Ditch	Antler	4310+/-110	3339-2626
WILTSHIRE					
Coneybury Anomaly	OxA-1402	Primary deposit	Bone	5050+/-100	4040-3640
South Street	BM-356	Buried soil beneath mound	Charcoal (oak)	4760+/-130	3910-3104
	BM-357	Ditch (base)	Bone (Bos)	4700+/-135	3767-3030
	BM-358a	Ditch (base)	Antler (red deer)	4620+/-140	3651-2931
	BM-358b	Mound (bay IIN)	Antler (red deer)	4530+/-110	3520-2919
Beckhampton Road	NPL-138	Beneath buried surface	Charcoal (oak)	5200+/-160	4344-3694
	BM-506b	Buried surface (bay XVII)	Antler (red deer)	4467+/-90	3369-2910
	BM-506a	Buried surface (bay XVII)	Antler (red deer)	4257+/-90	3101-2575
Easton Down	Ox A-3759	Buried turf line	Bone (bos)	4610+/-60	3600-3105
	Ox A3760	Primary silt ditch	Antler (red deer)	4730+/-65	3690-3360
	Ox A 3762	Primary silt ditch	Tooth (red deer)	4535+/-65	3495-3030
	OxA-3761	Upper secondary ditch	Tooth (bos)	3860+/-60	2555-2142
Normanton Down	BM-505	Bedding trench	Antler		3510-2920
West Kennet	OxA-449	NW chamber	Human skull	4825+/-90	3783-3373
	OxA-451	SW chamber	Human bone	4780+/-90	3709-3363
	OxA-563	NW chamber	Human bone	4780+/-90	3709-3363
	OxA-450	NE chamber	Human bone	4700+/-80	3646-3345
Netheravon Bake	OxA-1407	Ditch phase 1	Antler	4760+/-90	3776-3350

Fussell's Lodge	BM-134	Primary burial	Charcoal	5180+/-150	4331-3696
Horslip	BM-180	Primary ditch	Antler	5190+/-150	4335-3700
Lesser Cursus	OxA-1404	Ditch phase 2			3642-2920
	OxA-1405	Ditch phase 1			3640-3044
Stonehenge Cursus	OxA-1403		Antler		2910-2460
Stonehenge	OxA-4902	Sarsen hole 27	Bone		4345-3979
YORKSHIRE					
Hanging Grimston	HAR-2160	Façade trench	Bone (pig)	4710+/-90	3671-3127
Ling Howe, Walkington	HAR-9248	Old ground surface	Charcoal	5220+/-100	4322-3798
Kemp Howe, Kowlams	HAR-8778	Façade trench	Charcoal	4870+/-90	3939-3378
Seamer Moor	HAR-8785	Hearth beneath mound	Charcoal	5260+/-100	4334-3811
	HAR-8786	Grave pit	Charcoal	4990+/-90	3965-3640
East Heslerton	HAR-7029	Façade trench	Charcoal	4920+/-90	3951-3525
	HAR-7030	Façade trench	Charcoal from post	5020=/-70	3961-3661
	HAR-7031	Façade trench	Charcoal	5020=/-110	4060-3633
	HAR-7032	Façade trench	Charcoal from post	4640+/-70	3635-3112
Street House, Loftus	BM1966R	Plank	Charcoal	4940=/-110	3975-3517
	BM-2013R	Façade trench	Charcoal	4840=/-130	3945-3365
	BM-2014R	Façade trench	Charcoal	4970+/-120	4040-3519
	BM-2060R	Mortuary structure	Charcoal	4480=/-160	3635-2761

BIBLIOGRAPHY

Albarella, U. 2006. 'Animals in the Neolithic: A Research Agenda? No Thanks', in D. Serjeantson and D. Field (eds) *Animals in the Neolithic of Britain and Europe,* Neolithic Studies Group Seminar Papers 7 Oxford: Oxbow

Aldsworth, F. G. 1973-4. *Towards a pre-Domesday geography of Hampshire: a review of the evidence,* BA dissertation, University of Southampton

Allcroft, H. 1908. *Earthwork of England* London: Macmillan & Co.

Anon. 1866. '…observations respecting tumuli in North Wiltshire' *Proceedings Society of Antiquaries* 2nd series, **3**, 215

Anon. 1920. (O.G.S. Crawford exhibited) *Proceedings of the Society of Antiquaries* **23**, 90-1

Anon. 1961. 'Supposed Barrow in Dunham New Park' *Journal Chester and Wales Archaeological Society* **48**, 45

Anon. 1968. 'Kemp Howe' *Ministry of Public Building and Works. Annual Report. Archaeological Excavations 1968* London: HMSO

Anon. 1974. 'Bedhampton, Camp Down, Bevis Grave' *Department of the Environment Archaeological Excavations 1974* London: HMSO

Anon. 1975. 'Bedhampton, Camp Down, Bevis Grave' *Department of the Environment Archaeological Excavations 1975* London: HMSO

Anon. 2001. 'Yarnton' *Current Archaeology* **173**, 216-221

Ashbee, P. 1966. 'The Fussell's Lodge Long Barrow Excavations 1957' *Archaeologia* **100**, 1-80

Ashbee, P. 1976. 'Bant's Carn, St Mary's, Isles of Scilly: An Entrance Grave Restored and Reconsiderd' *Cornish Archaeology* **15**, 11-26

Ashbee, P., Smith, I.F. and Evans, J.G. 1979. 'Excavation of Three Long Barrows near Avebury, Wiltshire' *Proceedings of the Prehistoric Society* **45**, 207-300

Atkinson, J.J.C., Piggott, C.M. and Sanders, N.K. 1951. *Excavations at Dorchester, Oxon* Oxford: Ashmolean Museum

Atkinson, R.J.C. 1965. 'Wayland's Smithy' *Antiquity* **39**, 126-33

Bamford, H. 1985. *Briar Hill excavation 1974-1978* Northampton: Northampton Development Corporation

Barclay, A. 2014. 'Re-dating the Coneybury Anomaly and its Implications for Understanding the Earliest Neolithic Pottery', *PAST* **77**, 11-13

Barclay, G.J. and Maxwell, G.S. *The Cleaven Dyke and Littleour* Edinburgh: Society of Antiquaries of Scotland

Barton, N.E., Berridge, P.J, Walker, M.J.C. and Bevins, R.E. 1995. 'Persistent Places in the Mesolithic Landscape: an example from the Black Mountain Uplands of South Wales' *Proceedings of the Prehistoric Society* **61**, 81-116

Barrett, J., Bradley R. and Green, M. 1991. *Landscape, Monuments and Society: the Prehistory of Cranborne Chase* Cambridge: Cambridge University Press

Bayliss, A. and Whittle, A. (eds) 'Histories of the Dead: building chronologies for five southern British long barrows', *Cambridge Archeological Journal* 17, Supplement

Benson, D. and Whittle, A. (eds) 2006 *Building Memories: the Neolithic Cotswold long barrow at Ascott-under-Wychwood, Oxfordshire*, Oxford: Oxbow

Bowden, M. 1991. *Pitt-Rivers* Cambridge: Cambridge University Press

Bradley, R. 1983. 'The Bank Barrows and Related Monuments of Dorset in the Light of Recent Fieldwork' *Proceedings Dorset Natural History and Archaeological Society* **105**, 15-20

Bradley, R 2002. *The Past in Prehistoric Societies* London & New York: Routledge

Bradley, R. and Chambers, R. 1988. 'A new study of the cursus complex at Dorchester on Thames' *Oxford Archaeological Journal* **7**(3), 271-89

Bradley, R. and Entwistle, R. 1985. 'Thickthorn Down long barrow – a new assessment' *Proceedings Dorset Natural History and Archaeological Society* **107**, 174-6

Brown, A., 2007, 'Dating the Onset of Cereal Cultivation in Britain and Ireland: the evidence from charred cereal grain', *Antiquity* **81**, 1042-1052

Brown, G., Field, D. and McOmish, D. 2005. *The Avebury Landscape: aspects of the field archaeology of the Marlborough Downs* Oxford: Oxbow

Buckley, D., Major, H. and Milton, B. 1988. 'Excavation of a possible Neolithic long barrow or Mortuary Enclosure at Rivenhall, Essex', 1986 *Proceedings of the Prehistoric Society* **54**, 77-92

Burl, A. and Mortimer, N. 2005. *Stukeley's Stonehenge An unpublished Manuscript 1721-1724* New Haven & London: Yale University Press

Calado, M. 2002. 'Standing stones and natural outcrops: the role of ritual monuments in the Neolithic transition of the Central Alentejo', C. Scarre (ed.) *Monuments and Landscape in Atlantic Europe*, 17-35 London & New York: Routledge

Carmichael, D. L., Hubert, J., Reeves, B. and Schanche, A. 1994. *Sacred Sites, Sacred Places* London & New York: Routledge

Case, H.J. 1982. 'The linear ditches and southern enclosure, North Stoke', in H.J. Case and A.W.R. Whittle (eds) *Settlement patterns in the Oxford Region: excavations at the Abingdon causewayed enclosure and other sites*, 60-75 Council for British Archaeology Research Volume 44

Chapman, R. 1981. 'The emergence of formal dispersal areas and the 'problem' of megalithic tombs', R. Chapman, I. Kinnes and K. Randborg (eds) *The Archaeology of Death,* 71-82 Cambridge: Cambridge University Press

Clark, J.G.D. 1937. 'Earthen Long Barrows' *Proceedings of the Prehistoric Society* **3**, 173-5

Cleal, R. 2004. 'The Dating and Diversity of the Earliest Ceramics of Wessex and South-West England', in R. Cleal and J. Pollard (eds) *Monuments and Material Culture: papers in honour of an Avebury archaeologist,* 164-192 East Knoyle: HobNob Press

Cleal, R.M.J., Walker, K.E. and Montague, R. 1995. *Stonehenge and its landscape: Twentieth century excavations* London: English Heritage

Clutton-Brock, J. 1984. *Excavations at Grimes Graves Norfolk 1972-1976 Fascicule 1 Neolithic Antler Picks* London: British Museum

Collier, L., Hobbs B., Neighbour, T. and Strachan, R. 2003. 'Resistivity imaging survey of Capo Long Barrow, Aberdeenshire' *Scottish Arcaeological Internal Report* **6**. www.sair.org.uk

Conyngham, Lord A.D. 1849. 'Account of discoveries of barrows near Scarborough' *Journal British Archaeological Association* **4**, 101-7

Crawford, O.G.S. 1922. The Andover District: An account of Sheet 283 of the One-inch Ordnance map Oxford: Oxford University Press

Crawford O.G.S. 1938. 'Bank-Barrows' *Antiquity* **12**, 228-32

Crawford, O.G.S. and Keiller, A. 1928. *Wessex from the Air* Oxford: Clarendon Press

Crumley, C. 1999. 'Sacred Landscapes: Constructed and Conceptualised', W. Ashmore, and A. Bernard Knapp, (eds) *Archaeologies of Landscape: contemporary perspectives,* 270-6

Cummings, V. 2002. 'Between Mountains and Sea: a Reconsideration of the Neolithic Monuments of South-West Scotland' *Proceedings Prehistoric Society* **68**, 125-46

Cunnington, M. 1940. 'An Urn from Wexcombe Down' *Wiltshire Archaeological and Natural History Society Magazine* **49**, 164-5

Cunnington, R.H. 1975. *From Antiquary to Archaeologist* Princes Risborough: Shire Publications

Cunnington, W. 1889. 'Notes on Bowl's Barrow' *Wiltshire Archaeological & Natural History Society Magazine* **24**, 104-25

Darvill, T. 1997. 'Neolithic Landscapes: Identity and definition', in P. Topping (ed.) *Neolithic Landscapes*, Neolithic Studies Group Seminar Papers **2**, 1-13 Oxford: Oxbow

Darvill, T. 2004. 'Soft-Rock and Organic Tempering' in R. Cleal and J. Pollard (eds)

Monuments and Culture, 193-6 East Knoyle: HobNob Press

Davidson, J.L. and Henshall, A.S. 1989. *The Chambered Cairns of Orkney* Edinburgh: Edinburgh University Press

Davies, S.M., Stacey, L.C. and Woodward, J. 1985. 'Excavations at Allington Avenue, Fordington, Dorchester 1984/5 interim report' *Proceedings Dorset Natural History and Archaeological Society* **107**, 101-10

Defoe, D. 1724. *A tour through the whole island of Great Britain* (Penguin ed. rep. 1979) Harmondsworth: Penguin Books

Dick, O. Lawson 1949. *Aubrey's Brief Lives* (Penguin ed. 1972), Harmondsworth: Penguin

Dixon, P. 1988. 'The Neolithic settlements on Crickley Hill', in C. Burgess, P. Topping, C. Mordants and M. Maddison (eds) *Enclosures and Defences in the Neolithic of Western Europe*, 75-88 Oxford: British Archaeological Reports BAR (S) 403

Drew, C.D. and Piggott, S. 1936. 'The Excavation of Long Barrow 163a on Thickthorn Down, Dorset' *Proceedings of the Prehistoric Society* **2**, 77-96

Drewett, P. 1975. 'The Excavation of an Oval Burial Mound of the Third Millennium BC at Alfriston, East Sussex, 1974' *Proceedings of the Prehistoric Society* **41**, 119-52

Drewett, P. 1986. 'The excavation of a Neolithic oval barrow at North Marden, West Sussex, 1982' *Proceedings Prehistoric Society* **52**, 31-52

Eagles, B. and Field, D. 2004. 'William Cunnington and the long barrows of the River Wylye', in R. Cleal and J. Pollard (eds) *Monuments and Material Culture* East Knoyle: HobNob Press

Eedle, M. de G. 1971. 'Street Cleansing and Refuse Collection from the Sixteenth Century to the Nineteenth Century (with special reference to Surrey)' *Surrey Archaeological Collections* **68**, 161-81

Evans, C. 1988. 'Acts of Enclosure: a consideration of concentrically organised causewayed enclosures', in J. Barrett and I. Kinnes (eds) *The Archaeology of Context: Recent Trends* Sheffield: University of Sheffield

Evans, C. and Hodder, I., 2006, *A Woodland Archeology: Neolithic Sites at Haddenham*, Oxford: Oxbow

Evans, J.G. and Simpson, D.D.A. 1991. 'Giants Hills 2 Long Barrow, Skendleby, Lincolnshire' *Archaeologia* **109**, 1-46

Field, D. 1984. 'Neolithic and Bronze Age ground stone implements from Surrey: morphology, petrology and distribution' *Surrey Archaeological Collections* **75**, 85-110

Fenner, V. 1994, *The Thames Valley Project: a report for the NMP*, Swindon: English Heritage

Fowles, J. (ed.) 1980. *John Aubrey's Monumenta Britannica* (compiled 1665-1693) annotated R. Legg Sherborne: Dorset Publishing Co.

French, C., Lewis, H., Allen, M.J., Scaife, R.G. and Green, M. 2003. 'Archaeological and Paleao-environmental Investigations of the Upper Allen Valley, Cranborne Chase, Dorset (1998-2000): a New Model of Earlier Holocene Landscape Development' *Proceedings of the Prehistoric Society* **69**, 201-34

French, C, Lewis, H, Allen, M, Green, M, Scaife, R and Gardiner, J, 2007, *Prehistoric Landscape Development and Human Impact in the Upper Allen Valley, Cranborne Chase, Dorset*, Cambridge: McDonald Institute for Archeological Research

Gibson, A. and Kinnes, I 1997. On the urns of a dilemma: radiocarbon and the Peterborough problem *Oxford Journal of Archaeology* **16**(1), 65-72

Green, M. 2000. *A landscape revealed: 10,000 years on a chalkland farm* Stroud: Tempus

Green, M. and Allen, M. 1997. 'An Early Prehistoric Shaft in Cranborne Chase' *Oxford Journal of Archaeology* **16**, 2, 121-32

Greenwell, Rev. W. 1865. 'Notices of the examination of ancient grave-hills in the North Riding of Yorkshire' *Archaeological Journal* **22**, 97-117

Greenwell, Rev. 1877. *British Barrows: a record of the examination of sepulchral mounds in various parts of England* Oxford: Clarendon Press

Grimes, W.F. 1960. *Excavations on defence sites 1939-1945* HMSO: London

Grinsell, L. 1957. 'Archaeological Gazetteer', in R.B. Pugh and E. Crittall, (eds) *A History of Wiltshire* I, pt I (Victoria County History) Oxford: Oxford University Press

Grinsell, L. 1976. *Folklore of prehistoric sites in Britain* Newton Abbot: David & Charles

Grundy, G.B. 1920. 'Saxon Land Charters of Wiltshire' *Archaeological Journal* **77**, 8-126

Head, Rev. Mr 1773. 'An Account of Some Antiquities discovered on digging into a large Roman Barrow at Elenborough, in Cumberland, 1763' *Archaeologia* **2**, 54-7

Hey, G. 1997. 'Neolithic settlement at Yarnton, Oxfordshire', in P. Topping (ed.) *Neolithic Landscapes: Neolithic Studies Group Seminar Papers* **2**, 98-111 Oxford: Oxbow

Hey, G, Dennis, C. and Mayes, A, 2007, 'Archeological Investigations on Whiteleaf Hill, Princes Risborough, Buckinghamshire, 2002-6', *Records of Bucks* **47**, pt 2, 1-80

Hodder, I. and Shand, P. 1988. 'The Haddenham long barrow: an interim statement' *Antiquity* **62**, 349-53

Hogg, A.H.A. 1941. 'A Long Barrow at West Rudham, Norfolk' *Norfolk Archaeology* **27**, 314-31

Humphrey, C. 1995. 'Chiefly and Shamanist Landscapes in Mongolia', in Hirsh, E. and O'Hanlon, M. (eds) *The Anthropology of Landscape: perspectives on Place and Space* 135-62 Oxford: Clarendon Press

Ingold, T. 2000. *The Perception of the Environment: essays in livelihood, dwelling, and skill* London & New York: Routledge

Issac, G. 1981. 'Stone Age visiting cards: approaches to the study of early land-use patterns, in I. Hodder, G. Isaac and M. Hammond (eds) *Patterns of the Past: studies in honour of David Clarke* Cambridge: Cambridge University Press

Jackson, J.E. 1862. *John Aubrey's Wiltshire: Topographical Collections* Devizes: Wiltshire Natural History and Archaeological Society

Jessup, R.F. 1937. 'Excavations at Jullieberrie's Grave, Chilham, Kent' *Antiquaries Journal* **17**, 122–37

Jessup, R.F. 1939. 'Further excavations at Jullieberrie's Grave, Chilham' *Antiquaries Journal* **19**, 260–81

Johnson, W. and Wright, W. 1903. *Neolithic Man in North East Surrey* London: Elliott Stock

Jones, A. 1998. Where Eagles Dare: landscape, animals and the Neolithic of Orkney *Journal of Material Culture* **3**, 301–324

Jones, D. 1998. 'Long Barrows and Neolithic Elongated Enclosures in Lincolnshire: An Analysis of the Air Photographic Evidence' *Proceedings Prehistoric Society* **64**, 83–114

Jordon, P.D. 2001. 'Cultural Landscapes in Colonial Siberia: Khanty Settlements of the Sacred, the Living and the Dead' *Landscapes* **2**, 2, 83–105

Keiller, A. and Piggott, S. 1939. 'Badshot Long barrow', in K. P. Oakley, W. F. Rankine and A. W. G. Lowther (eds) *A Survey of the Prehistory of the Farnham District (Surrey)*, 133–49 Guildford: Surrey Archaeological Society

Kenwood, R. 1982. 'A Neolithic burial enclosure at New Wintles Farm, Eynsham', in H.J. Case and A.W.R. Whittle (eds) *Settlement patterns in the Oxford Region: excavations at the Abingdon causewayed enclosure and other sites*, 51–4 Council for British Archaeology Research Volume 44

Kinnes, I. 1979. *Round Barrows and Ring Ditches in the British Neolithic* British Museum Occasional Paper 7

Kinnes, I. 1992. *Non-Megalithic Long Barrows and Allied Structures in the British Neolithic* British Museum Occasional Paper 52

Kinnes, I.A. and Longworth, I.H. 1985. *Catalogue of the excavated Prehistoric and Roman-British material in the Greenwell Collection* London: British Museum

Kristiansen, K 1990. 'Ard marks under barrows: a response to Peter Rowly-Conwy' *Antiquity* **64**, 322–7

Lambert, A.B. 1806. 'Further account of tumuli opened in Wiltshire in a letter from Mr William Cunnington to Aylmer Bourke Lambert' *Archaeologia* **15**, 338–46

Leary, J. 2015, *The Remembered Land: surviving sea-level rise after the last Ice Age*, London: Bloomsbury

Legge, A. J. 1991 'The Animal Remains from Six Sites at Down Farm, Woodcutts', in J. Barrett, R. Bradley and M. Hall (eds) *Papers on the Prehistoric Archaeology of Cranborne Chase* Oxford: Oxbow

Long, A.J. and Roberts, D.H. 1997. Sea-level change, in M. Fulford, T. Champion and
    A. Long (eds) *England's coastal heritage*, 25-49 RCHME and English Heritage
Loveday, R. and Petchey, M. 1983. 'Oblong ditches: A Discussion and Some New
    Evidence' *Aerial Archaeology* **8**, 17-24

MacDonald, J. 1976. 'Neolithic', *The Archaeology of the London Area: Current Knowledge
    and Problems* London and Middlesex Archaeological Soc Special Paper 1, 19-32
Madsen, T. 1979. 'Earthen Long Barrows and Timber Structures: Aspects of the Early
    Neolithic Mortuary Practice in Denmark' *Proceedings of the Prehistoric Society* **45**,
    301-20
Manby, T. 1963. 'The excavation of the Willerby Wold long barrow, East Riding of
    Yorkshire, England' *Proceedings of the Prehistoric Society* **29**, 173-205
Manby, T. 1976. 'The excavation of Kilham long barrow, East Riding of Yorkshire'
    Proceedings of the Prehistoric Society **42**, 111-60
Manby, T.G. 1988. 'The Neolithic Period in Eastern Yorkshire', in T.G. Manby (ed.)
    Archaeology in Eastern Yorkshire: Essays in Honour of T. C. M. Brewster FSA, 35-88
    Sheffield: Department of Archaeology and Prehistory
McOmish, D., Field, D. and Brown, G. 2002. *The field archaeology of Salisbury Plain
    Training Area* Swindon: English Heritage
Megaw, J.V.S. 1976. 'Gwithian, Cornwall: some notes on the evidence for Neolithic and
    Bronze Age settlement', in C. Burgess and R. Miket (eds) In *Settlement and Economy in
    the Third and Second Millennia BC,* 51-80 Oxford: British Archaeological Reports 33
Mercer, R.J. 1981. 'Excavations at Carn Brae, Illogen, Cornwall, 1970-73' *Cornish
    Archaeology* **20**, 1-204
Miles, D. and Palmer, S. 1993. 'In search of the White Horse' *Oxford Archaeological Unit
    Annual Report 1993-4*
Morgan, F. de M. 1959. 'The Excavation of a Long Barrow at Nutbane, Hants'
    Proceedings of the Prehistoric Society **25**, 15-51
Morgan, V. and Morgan P. 2004. *Prehistoric Cheshire* Ashbourne: Landmark Publishing

Ordnance Survey 1932. *Map of Neolithic Wessex* Southampton: Ordnance Survey Office
Oswald, A. 2001. *The Creation of Monuments* Swindon: English Heritage

Parker Pearson, M. and Ramilisonina 1998. Stonehenge for the Ancestors: the stones
    pass on the message *Antiquity* **72**, 308-26 and 855-6
Payne, A. 2000. *White Barrow, Tilshead 4 Long Barrow, Tilshead, Wilts Report on Geophysical
    Surveys, May 1997* English Heritage Ancient Monuments Laboratory Report No 70/2000
Pegg, Rev. 1785. 'Disquisition on the Lows or barrows in the Peak of Derbyshire'
    Archaeologia **7**, 131-48
Phillips, C.W. 1935. 'A Re-examination of the Therfield Heath long barrow, Royston,

Hertfordshire' *Proceedings of the Prehistoric Society* **1**, 101-107

Phillips, C.W. 1936. 'The Excavation of the Giants Hills Long Barrow, Skendleby, Lincolnshire' *Archaeologia* **85**, 37-106

Piggott, S. 1935. 'A Note on the Relative Chronology of the English Long Barrow' *Proceedings of the Prehistoric Society* **1**, 115-126

Piggott, S. 1937a. 'The Excavation of a Long Barrow in Holdenhurst Parish, near Christchurch, Hampshire' *Proceedings of the Prehistoric Society* **3**, 1-14

Piggott, S. 1937b. 'The Long Barrow in Brittany' *Antiquity* **11** (44), 441-55

Piggott, S. 1955. 'Windmill Hill – East or West' *Proceedings of the Prehistoric Society* 21, 96-107

Piggott, S. 1962a. *The West Kennet long barrow: Excavations 1955-56* London: HMSO

Piggott, S 1962b. 'Heads and Hoofs' *Antiquity* **36**, 110-18

Piggott, S. 1967. ''Unchambered' long barrows in Neolithic Britain' *Palaeohistoria* **12** (1966)

Piggott, S. 1972. 'Excavation of the Dalladies long barrow, Fettercairn, Kincardineshire' *Proc Soc Ant Scot* **104**, 23-47

Piggott, S. 1973. 'The Dalladies long barrow: Northeast Scotland' *Antiquity* **47**, 32-411 Dalladies

Piggott, S. 1991. 'The Background and Beginnings of the Wiltshire Archaeological and Natural History Society' *Wiltshire Archaeological and Natural History Society Magazine* **84**, 108-15

Piggott, S. 1993. 'John Thurnam (1810-1873) and British Prehistory' *Wiltshire Archaeological and Natural History Magazine* **86**, 1-7

Pitt Rivers, A. H. L. 1898 *Excavations in Cranborne Chase* **4** Privately Printed

Pollard, J. and Reynolds, A. 2002. *Avebury: The biography of a landscape* Stroud: Tempus

Powell, T.G.E., Fell, C.I., Corcoran, J.X.W.P. and Barnes, F. 1963. 'Excavations at Skelmore Heads near Ulverston, 1957 and 1959' *Transactions Cumberland and Westmorland Antiquarian and Archaeological Society* **63**, 1-30

Rawlings, M., Allen, M. and Healy, F. 2004. 'Investigation of the Whitesheet Hill Environs 1988-90: Neolithic Causewayed Enclosure and Iron Age Settlement' *Wiltshire Archaeological and natural History Society Magazine* **97**, 106-43

RCHME 1979a. *Long Barrows in Hampshire and the Isle of Wight* London: HMSO

RCHME 1979b. *Stonehenge and its environs: monuments and land-use* Edinburgh: Edinburgh University Press

RCHME 1989. *The classification of crop marks in Kent* London: RCHME

RCHME 1997. *Ancient landscapes of the Yorkshire Wolds* Swindon: HMSO

Renfrew, C. 1973. 'Monuments, mobility and social organisation in Neolithic Wessex', in C. Renfrew (ed.) *The explanation of culture change: models in prehistory*, 539-588 London: Duckworth

Richards, J. 1990. *The Stonehenge Environs Project* London: HBMC

Richards, M.P. and Hedges, R.E.M. 1999. 'A Neolithic revolution? New evidence of diet in the British Neolithic' *Antiquity* **73**, 891-7

Ridgeway, V. 1999. 'Prehistoric finds at Hopton Street in Southwark' *London Archaeologist* **9**: No 3, 72-6.

Riley, D.N. 1988. 'Air survey at Neolithic sites in the Yorkshire Wolds', in T.G. Manby (ed.) *Archaeology in Eastern Yorkshire: Essays in Honour of T.C.M. Brewster FSA*, 89-93 Sheffield: Department of Archaeology and Prehistory

Ross Williamson, R.B. 1930. 'Excavations in Whitehawk Neolithic Camp, near Brighton' *Sussex Archaeological Collections* **71**, 56-96

Rowley Conwy P. 1987. 'The interpretation of ard marks' *Antiquity* **61**, 263-66

Saville, A. 1990. *Hazleton North: The excavation of a Neolithic long cairn of the Cotswold-Severn Group* London: HBMC

Schuldt, E. 1972. *Die mecklenburgisen megalithgräber* Berlin: VED Deutches Verlag der Wissenschaften

Schulting, R. 2000. 'New AMS dates from the Lambourn Long barrow and the question of the earliest Neolithic in Southern England: Repacking the Neolithic package?' *Oxford Journal Archaeology* **19**, 25-35

Schulting, R. 2002. 'Cranial Trauma in the British Neolithic' *PAST* **41**, 4-6

Schulting, R. and Wysocki, M. 2005. 'In this Chambered Tumulus were Found Cleft Skulls...' An Assessment of the Evidence for Cranial Trauma in the British Neolithic *Proceedings of the Prehistoric Society* **71**, 107-38

Serjeantson, D. 2006. 'Food or Feast at Neolithic Runnymede' in D. Serjeantson and D. Field (eds) *Animals in the Neolithic of Britain and Europe: Neolithic Studies Group Seminar Papers* **7**, 113-34

Sharples, N. 2000. 'Antlers and Orcadian rituals: an Ambiguous Role for Red Deer in the Neolithic' in A. Ritchie (ed.) *Neolithic Orkney in its European Context* Cambridge: MacDonald Inst Mon

Shepherd, I.A.G. 1976. 'Preliminary results from the Beaker settlement at Rosinith, Benbecula', in C. Burgess and R. Miket (eds) *Settlement and Economy in the Third and Second Millennia BC* 209-219 Oxford: British Archaeological Reports 33

Shepherd, I.A.G., and Tuckwell, A.N. 1977. 'Traces of Beaker Period Cultivation at Rosinish, Benbecula' *Proceedings of the Society of Antiquaries of Scotland* **108**, 108-13.

Simpson, D.D.A. 1971. 'Beaker houses and settlements in Britain', in D.D.A. Simpson (ed.) *Economy and settlement in Neolithic and Early Bronze Age Britain and Europe* 131-152 Leicester: Leicester University Press.

Smith, M. and Brickley, M, 2009, *People of the Long Barrows; life, death and burial in the earlier Neolithic*, Stroud: The History Press

Smith, Rev. A.C. 1884. *Guide to the British and Roman Antiquities of north Wiltshire* Marlborough: Marlborough College Natural History Society

Snead, J.E. and Preucel, R.W. 1999. 'The Ideology of Settlement: Ancestral Keres Landscapes in the Northern Rio Grande', in W. Ashmore and A. Bernard Knapp (eds) *Archaeologies of Landscape: contemporary perspectives*, 169-97 Oxford & Massachusetts: Blackwell

Stukeley, W. 1740. *Stonehenge, a temple Restor'd to the British Druids* London: Innys & Manby

Stukeley, W. 1743. *Avebury, a temple of the British Druids* London

Stukeley, W. 1776. *Itinerarium Curiosum* 2nd ed. London: Baker & Leigh

Sumner, H. 1913. *The Ancient Earthworks of Cranborne Chase*

Taylor, C. 1972. 'The study of settlement patterns in pre-Saxon Britain', in P. Ucko, R. Tringham and G. Dimbleby (eds) *Man, settlement and urbanism,* 109-13 London: Duckworth

Theodoratus, D. J. and Lapena, F. 1994. 'Wintu Sacred Geography of Northern California', in D.L. Carmichael, J. Hubert, B. Reeves and A. Schanche (eds) *Sacred Sites, Sacred Places*, 20-31 London & New York: Routledge

Thorpe, I. J. 1984. 'Ritual, power and ideology: a reconstruction of earlier Neolithic rituals in Wessex', in R. Bradley and J. Gardiner (eds) *Neolithic Studies: A Review of Some Current Research*, 41-60 Oxford: British Archaeological Reports 133

Thurnam, J. 1855. 'On the barrow at Lanhill near Chippenham' *Wiltshire Archaeological & Natural History Society Magazine* **3**, 67-86

Thurnam, J. 1864. '…exhibited four flint implements' *Proceedings of the Society of Antiquaries* 2nd series 2, 427-31

Thurnam J. 1869. 'On Ancient British Barrows, especially those of Wiltshire and the adjoining Counties (Part I-Long barrows)' *Archaeologia* **42**, 161-244

Thurnam J. 1871. 'On Ancient British barrows, especially those of Wiltshire and the adjoining Counties (Part 2-Round barrows)' *Archaeologia* **43**, 285-544

Tilley, C. 1994. *A phenomenology of landscape* Oxford: Berg

Toms, H.S. 1922. 'Long Barrows in Sussex' *Sussex Archaeological Collections* **63**, 157-65

Topping, P. 1997. 'Structured deposition, symbolism and the English flint mines', in R. Schild and Z. Sulgostowska (eds) *Man and Flint*, 127-132 Warsaw: Institute of Archaeology and Ethnology. Polish Academy of Sciences

Topping, P. 2005. 'Shaft 27 Revisited: An Ethnography of Neolithic Flint Extraction', in P. Topping and M. Lynott (eds) *The Cultural Landscape of Prehistoric Mines*, 63-93 Oxford: Oxbow

Turner, D. 1997. 'Pipeline from Lavant' in S. Woodward (ed.) *The Archaeology of Chichester and District 1997.* Southern Archaeology Annual Report. Chichester: Chichester District Council

Turner, E. 1863. Rottingdean *Sussex Archaeological Collections* **15**, 243-4

Vatcher, F. de M. and H.L. 1965. 'East Heslerton long barrow, Yorkshire: The Eastern Half' *Antiquity* **39**, 49-52

Vyner, B.E. 1984. 'The Excavation of Neolithic Cairn at Street House, Loftus, Cleveland' *Proceedings of the Prehistoric Society* **50**, 151-95

Waddington, C. 2003. 'Howick and East barns' *Current Archaeology* **189**, 394-9

Warne, C. 1866. *The Celtic Tumuli of Dorset* London: John Russell Smith

Welfare, H. 1989. 'John Aubrey – The first archaeological surveyor?', in M. Bowden, D. Mackay and P. Topping (eds) *From Cornwall to Caithness: some aspects of British Field Archaeology* British Archaeological Reports 209

Whittle, A, 1991, 'Waylands Smithy, Oxfordshire: excavations at the Neolithic tomb in 1962-3 by RJC Atkinson and S Piggott', *Proceedings Prehistoric Society* **57** (2), 61-101

Whittle, A. 1993. 'The Neolithic of the Avebury area: sequence, environment, settlement and monuments' *Oxford Journal Archaeology* **12**, 29-53

Whittle, A., Atkinson, R.J.C., Chambers, R. and Thomas, N. 1992. 'Excavations in the Neolithic and Bronze Age Complex at Dorchester-on-Thames, Oxfordshire, 1947-1952 and 1981' *Proceedings of the Prehistoric Society* **58**, 143-202

Whittle, A. and Healy, F. and Bayliss, A, 2011, *Gathering Time: dating the early Neolithic enclosures of southern Britain and Ireland*, Oxford: Oxbow

Whittle, A., Rouse, A.J. and Evans, J.G. 1993. 'A Neolithic downland monument in its environment: excavations at the Easton Down Long Barrow, Bishops Cannings, north Wiltshire' *Proceedings of the Prehistoric Society* **59**, 197-240

Williams, J.L., Davidson, A., Flook, R, Jenkins, D.A., Muckle, P. and Roberts, T. 1998. 'Survey and excavation at the Graiglwyd Neolithic axe-factory, Penmaenmawr' Archaeology in Wales **38**, 3-21

Windell, D., Chapman, A. and Woodiwiss, J. 1990. *From barrow to bypass: Excavations at West Cotton, Raunds, Northamptonshire, 1985-1989* Northampton: Northamptonshire County Council

Wingfield Gibbons, D., Reid, J.B., and Chapman R.A. 1993. *The New Atlas of Breeding Birds in Britain and Ireland: 1988-1991* London: T&AD Poyser Ltd

Woodward, P. 1978. 'Flint distribution, ring ditches and Bronze Age settlement patterns in the Great Ouse Valley' *Archaeological Journal* **135**, 32-56

Young, R. 1980. 'An Inventory of the Barrows in Co. Durham' *Transactions Architectural and Archaeological Society of Durham and Northumberland* **5**, 1-16

INDEX